Mystic Pathways through The Bible

Swami Jyotirmayananda

YOGA RESEARCH FOUNDATION

CENTER FOR INTEGRAL YOGA

AIMS AND OBJECTIVES

1. To disseminate the essence and mystical meaning of all *Vedantic* Scriptures and the Scriptures of the world, revealing thereby that "Truth is One - Sages and Saints speak of it in different ways."

2. To emphasize the oneness in Creation and cultivate a Spirit that communes with the Ocean of Universal Awareness in the spirit of the *Vedantic* axiom - *"Vasudeva Kutumbakam"* - this world is our family.

3. To introduce to the world the time-proven philosophy of Integral Yoga to bring about the highest culture that humanity can attain.

4. To serve humanity by raising human consciousness through teaching the technique of mastering the mind and following the principles of "simple living and high thinking."

5. To promote the understanding that the ultimate purpose of life is Self-Realization, and to offer powerful and time-tested techniques for attaining it.

6. To demonstrate that one can live in this stressful world, and yet rise above it by learning to use every circumstance in one's life to their advantage.

7. To make available to all, the means to attain a healthy body through *Hatha Yoga* exercises, and *Pranayama* (techniques for breathing correctly).

8. To train the mind to be focused, peaceful, and relaxed, and to go beyond self-limiting concepts in order to discover one's infinite potential.

9. To teach the art of meditation to enable one to render the mind acquiescent, and ultimately to learn how to transcend the body and the mind to experience the super-conscious state of *samadhi*.

10. To publish and make available through books and all media possible, teachings of the highest order, drawn from the ancient wisdom of *Vedanta*, and expressed with rare intuition by the Spiritual Master— Sri Swami Jyotirmayananda.

Mystic Pathways through the Bible
Copyright © 2018 by Swami Jyotirmayananda
All rights reserved.

Yoga Research Foundation
6111 S.W. 74th Avenue
Miami, Florida 33143 U.S.A.
Tel: (305) 666-2006 • www.yrf.org

ISBN: 978-0-934664-13-4
Library of Congress Catalog Card Number 94-060938

Cover and Interior Design: Sushila Oliphant

Editors: Daya Callan and Swami Umananda

Illustrations: Doré Etchings, Sushila Oliphant and the oil painting of Christ Madhava (Bob Stuth-Wade)

Printed in the United States

Table of Contents

Introduction
Truth Is One

The Vedas say, *"Ekam Sat Vipra Bahudha Vadanti"*—"Truth is one, but Sages speak of it in different ways." All religions and spiritual denominations lead one to the same Divine Self, but in ways that are beautifully unique. Every religion resembles a cherished garden that contains a variety of special flowers. You may have your own garden and truly enjoy the beautiful elegance of its blossoms and foliage. Yet when you are invited by your neighbor to see his garden, you also admire the magnificence of his collection as well. After visiting, you might even return home with an assortment of plants from his garden. The beauty that expresses in both gardens is ultimately the same. Similarly, every religion leads you in its own artistic way to the same awareness of Divine beauty and Truth.

It is due to the lack of this most important understanding that so much dissention, strife and bloodshed have been promoted in the name of religion. If properly understood, religion leads one not to disharmony, but to Divine Love. Sri Ramakrishna Paramhamsa, an Indian Saint of recent times, was a great exponent of the unity of religions. After intensely following the Biblical path, he experienced a vision of Lord Jesus. This vision enthralled him as much as a Hindu would be enraptured by the vision of Krishna. On another occasion, while continuing his spiritual quest, he was following the mystic teachings of the Koran, and the Divine Presence of Allah manifested. Thus, through his own direct mystical experiences, he gained intuitive understanding of how all religions eventually lead one to the same Truth. To him, the vision of Christ was just as inspiring as the vision of Allah; he saw no differences in the ultimate mystical experience of man's communion with the Supreme Self.

To help people understand that the various religions essentially express the same message, Sri Ramakrishna characterized this point in a parable: A number of thirsty people who all spoke different languages encountered each other in the middle of a desert. Finding themselves in a difficult predicament, each one began to clamor for water. The Arabic philosopher shouted, "Aab," the Englishman bellowed, "Water," the Hindu yelled, "Pani," the Sanskrit scholar cried out for "Jala," and the

Spaniard shouted, "Agua!" A colossal fight ensued in which each man asserted that what he thought was necessary was better than what the others wanted. This, of course, was ridiculous because they were all striving for the same goal—water in order to live.

Much in the same way, people of different religions are all inspired to move towards God. They receive the same inspirational message from their inner soul; however, the symbolic images of God differ. Some see Allah, others see Lord Krishna and still others see Lord Jesus. There are multiple symbols that devotees use throughout the world for the same God that exists within all. Each feels a profound satisfaction communicating with their particular Deity, and each is convinced that their Deity will quench their spiritual thirst for true happiness and security. However, what they do not understand is that everyone is communicating with the very same God manifesting in various forms.

Religious movements are found throughout the world because the human heart is intuitively drawn to the mystical realm that returns one to God, to one's real Home. The relative world is not enough for a human being, and ultimately each person intuitively knows that this world is only temporary. Therefore, we are inwardly driven to discover our relationship with God. When people turn to religion, they are turning to a realm of reality that cannot be completely understood by human reason. Exploring that realm requires faith, purification of heart and integration of personality. It is the thirst for that discovery of Truth that has led to the development of the world's great variety of philosophies and religions.

Differences among religions are apparent and not intrinsic. Conflicts exist because people are not able to understand the implied meaning in the scriptural writings. If worshippers comprehended the true spirit of their religion, they would view every other religion with great admiration.

Unfortunately, many priests and religious leaders do not encourage a deeper understanding of the scriptural texts. Rather, they encourage the belief that their own religion is the only one that teaches the Truth. As a result, more energy is devoted to proving the superiority of one's religion than to practicing its precepts. Divine Love, which ought to open the heart of man to the perception of universal unity, is thwarted. In its place a vague, superstitious, and biased faith emerges, which is the bane of many religions.

Worshippers who are sectarian in nature are unable to accept the fact that the Truth behind every religion is the same. Such worshippers are more dependent upon the religious system that has been presented by the churches, temples or mosques than they are upon the teachings of Christ revealed in the New Testament, or the teachings of Krishna in the

Bhagavad Gita, or the teachings of Mohammed in the Koran.

A ritualistic form of religion provides a good basis for a person's spiritual growth, but as spirituality grows, one's vision must transcend the barriers of all sects and creeds. It must recognize the fundamental unity behind all religious and mystical movements and should not be stifled by sectarian dogma and ritualism.

If a Hindu of simple education unknowingly reads a portion of the Bible, he might very well think that he was reading a portion of the Puranas. This is not really surprising, however, since Yoga is a universal science of mystic communion with the Divine Self. With this lofty understanding in mind, let us embark upon a study of selected topics that give insight into the mysticism of the Holy Bible in the light of Yoga and Vedanta philosophy.

Chapter One

The Ten Commandments

As described in Exodus in the Old Testament, after performing great austerity, Moses received the Ten Commandments from God as imprints on stone. These commandments are:

I. **I am the Lord thy God. Thou shalt not have other gods before me.**

II. **Thou shalt not make unto thee any graven image.**

III. **Thou shalt not take the name of the Lord, thy God, in vain.**

IV. **Remember the Sabbath Day to keep it holy.**

V. **Honor thy father and thy mother.**

VI. **Thou shalt not kill.**

VII. **Thou shalt not commit adultery.**

VIII. **Thou shalt not steal.**

IX. Thou shalt not bear false witness.

X. Thou shalt not covet.

The Ten Commandments became the rock and foundation of a powerful religious movement in Judaism and Christianity. When we study these commandments in the light of the Vedic culture, we discover their great importance in that culture as well. Indeed, if these commandments are properly understood, they can be seen to be of paramount importance in all religious and moral teachings.

Although the Ten Commandments are understood to be God's message, their deeper implications are hardly known or understood. Often they become dry ethical rules, simply to be committed to memory and rarely practiced. In the light of Yoga philosophy, you will be able to see the depth and profundity of these commandments. They imply a study of the very basic structure of the mind that leads to the development of virtues and a deep insight into the meaning of universal law.

The commandments must be well comprehended, not only by the individual, but by the world as well, because life must be founded on *dharma* or righteousness. The Sanskrit word *dharma* actually means "that which upholds." *Dharma* is a very significant term in Hindu as well as Buddhistic mysticism. Every Buddhist monk repeats,

"Dhammam sharanam gacchsami"—"I take refuge in *dharma*, in the moral order that sustains the world."

The first four commandments focus on the nature of God, the Divine Self, and one's relationship to God. They clearly point out that God is transcendental, nondual and beyond the mind and senses. These commandments also establish the creation of the sublime order of the world, in which God is the father, and Divine Nature is the mother; and we must listen sensitively to the commands of our Divine parents as we move about in the world.

The last six commandments are more subjective and relate to one's relationship to others and an understanding of the human personality. They are essentially the same as the *yamas* enumerated in Raja Yoga. The concept of *yama*, Yogic virtue, is very profound. It highlights the deeper attitudes that dominate the mind, rather than what one shows to another on the level of superficial words or actions. Furthermore, it leads to the understanding that a person cannot be established in one virtue unless all other virtues also unfold through integration of one's personality.

The commandments, therefore, are far more profound than they appear to be. They are not merely instructions. They are universal laws of the mind based upon the vision of Self-realization. Because of their importance, they constitute timeless ideals for guiding humanity through all eras.

First Commandment

I am the Lord thy God.
Thou shalt not have other gods before me.

This commandment is a declaration of the nonduality of existence—the nonduality of the Divine Self. If the Self, or God, is infinite, how can there be two Gods? There cannot be two infinities. God is One. God is nondual. There cannot be any God other than the Absolute Self. However, the commandment can often be misinterpreted by the masses to mean: *My God is the only God, and the God of other faiths is not the true God. The God of the Mohammedans, the God of the Hindus or the Zoroastrians are all satanic personalities!* This misinterpretation encouraged by some spiritual ministers has created so much dissension, hostility and hatred among the races of man and has resulted in terrible fighting in the name of religion.

Regarded in still another way, "other gods" refers to the concepts, names, and forms to which one becomes attached for selfish purposes, for perpetuating egoism, superiority and the sense of individuality or separation. In other words, when you insult another person's right to worship God in his or her own way, or disrespect a person's religion or spiritual practice, you are worshipping pettiness, criticism, and material objects alone. You are not worshipping God for the attainment of the Kingdom of Heaven and spiritual peace. You are worshipping "other gods."

A story from India illustrates this point. A simple farmer repeated the mantra of Kubera, the Hindu god of wealth. Pleased by the man's prayers, Kubera presented himself before the farmer and asked what boon he would like to receive. The farmer, whose vision was limited to only his everyday needs, said, "I need sixty large loads of straw for my animals." Since that was all he could think of, that was what he received from the limitless treasury of Kubera.

Similarly, when you worship God—the source and substratum of all that exists in the universe— for perishable, petty attainments, that is what you will receive. And as a result, what you attain will be little compared to what you could have received: the infinite expansion of the Self, which is your birthright.

Second Commandment

Thou shalt not make unto thee any graven image.

In prohibiting idolatry, this commandment points out the error in mentally trying to reduce God, Who is infinite and transcendental, to the level of name and form. The error is in trying to permanently bring God into the realm of relativity. However, the subtle meaning of the commandment is usually overlooked, and people try to interpret its words too literally. The commandment should not give you the wrong idea of suddenly renouncing every name and form for God. That cannot be done.

It is impossible for a person to worship God without having some concept to support the mind. Every human being is a born "idol worshipper" in the sense that he depends on symbols. Every thought is a form; every concept is a form and every movement requires a form to lean upon. The form may be concrete, or it may be abstract. Even the idea that God is without form creates a form in the mind of one who has not realized God.

Any limited name, form, or concept that you visualize as God can be considered an idol. If you consider God to be all-pervading, that concept can also be considered a psychological idol. If you consider God to be all-compassionate, you have again created a type of idol. If you worship God with any form that can be described or visualized, you are using a type of idol.

No matter how one may try to avoid all images in religious practice, all churches have them in one form or another. Even if you do not have any images in the church, the place of worship in itself is an image. No one in this world can suddenly go beyond all symbols in order to experience the Divine Self. Rather, one should use name and form in the worship of God, but at the same time maintain the understanding that the Divine Self is beyond all names and forms. Therefore, any attempt to limit God by names and forms is an error in thought.

The Difference between Idol Worship and Worshipping God through an Idol

Subtlety of reason is required to understand the difference between idolatry and worshipping God through an idol that one views as a symbol or medium for worship. In the Vedic tradition there is no idolatry. Every form in this tradition is a gateway to the Divine Self. When you worship Rama or Krishna or Lord Jesus, or any Sage or Saint, that object of your worship becomes a window to the Highest.

You are an idolater or an idol worshipper if you consider the idol itself to be the Ultimate Reality. You are not an idol worshipper if the idol is considered to be a symbol of the Absolute Reality. This second attitude towards idols is in no way a contradiction to the commandment. The error of idol worship does not lie in the use of concepts or symbols about God to enhance your worship. The error lies in adopting a biased attitude about God, in developing the notion that whatever concept or symbol you have relied upon is the only correct one and the only way God can be worshipped.

If you develop the idea that God can be worshipped only in Mecca or in Varanasi (Benares), or that the God of a particular religion is the only Living God and all other gods are insignificant or even satanic—then you are worshipping idols and you are an idolater. If you say, "Christ is the only one who can liberate you, and if you worship Buddha or Krishna you will go to hell!"—that is a form of idolatry.

The human mind conceives of God on the basis of its own concepts, and those concepts become obstructions when you do not rise above them. You invest certain value and power in those concepts and insist that others must adopt them as well. Throughout the centuries, everyone who has adored God in a particular form has wanted the whole of humanity to do the same. But there lies a great error. Without realizing it, you are turning away from the real God and running after the illusions of God. This can make it difficult or impossible for you to move towards God-realization.

There has been much discord in India between the people who believe God should be worshipped without form—the *nirakara* worshippers—and those who feel God should be worshipped with form—the *sakara* worshippers. Heated arguments developed, leading to misunderstanding, hatred and violence as each group attempted to prove that they were correct. However, both groups had really been worshipping idols by being attached to their mental concepts, when, in fact, God is beyond all of these.

There was a similar lack of deeper understanding by the masses when the Prophet Mohammed taught that God is beyond all idols. Because of this misinterpretation, followers destroyed places of worship and brutally massacred people who worshipped God while using forms and symbols.

However, while they were destroying what they felt were idols, they were creating other idols of their own at the very same time. They built mosques, and a mosque without anything in it is still an idol. Removing everything, or the negation of things, also becomes a form in itself.

All people who have renounced idol worship have themselves created idols in one way or another. They have often become degraded by such worship as well, because they became attached to their own physical or mental forms. This obstructs their ability to realize God, Who transcends all form.

Transcending Mental Symbols

No matter how great and inspiring the form of a Deity, Saint or Sage may be, that form itself will be spontaneously transcended when you attain higher levels of *samadhi* (superconsciousness) that lead you to God-realization or the Kingdom of Heaven. This Truth is made evident in the life of Sri Ramakrishna, when he became overly attached to the form of Goddess Kali. To facilitate Ramakrishna's attainment of Self-realization, his Guru encouraged him to immediately relinquish the form of Kali with the sword of discrimination each time she appeared before him in his meditation.

The conceptual God, who has inspired you throughout your spiritual journey, must eventually be left behind and transcended by your increasing discrimination. Although your mental concept of God has helped you up to that point, you must reach a stage in which you graduate beyond that concept and merge with God Who is beyond all mental forms. You cannot be confined to a mental fabrication of duality when entering into the infinite world of the Divine.

A mind that cannot expand to unify with God soon becomes a habitation for ignorance and darkness. On the other hand, if the *chitta* (mind) has an accurate understanding of Divine worship, then goodness and light will manifest within every aspect of your personality. Your intellect will be purified; your senses and mind will be healthy. Even your physical body will vibrate with higher forces of *prana* (vital energy). Therefore, abundance will proceed from God and lead you to attain the goal of life: God-realization.

Third Commandment

***Thou shalt not take the Name of
the Lord thy God in vain.***

This commandment urges a person not to take the Divine Name lightly. In daily conversation many people utter "Oh God," over the smallest problems or sources of frustration. Further, many swear when they are angry, invoking the name of God as if to give authority to their weakness and loss of mental balance. Some people even worship God in order to harm others, and some assert the name of God in perpetuating evil. In all of these cases, one is taking the name of God in vain.

Because God is infinite benevolence, you cannot call upon God or invoke His name for supporting your weaknesses or perpetuating any form of evil. On the other hand, repetition of mantra, using the name of God for advocating goodness, or adoring and glorifying Him through speech are all in perfect harmony with the commandment.

The Glory of the Divine Name

Further, this commandment is intended to convey the wondrous glory of the Divine name and to encourage *japa*, or the repetition of that name. Repeating the Divine name, in whatever form you choose, is one of the easiest and most powerful ways to capture the Absolute. It is a miraculous string that allows you to reach out to the Divine Self and tie Him down within your very heart. Thus, the science of *japa* has existed in one form or another in every religion from ancient times.

When a mantra, a Divine formula or prayer, is repeated with profound feeling and understanding of what it represents, the name of God is truly glorified. Each time the name of God is brought to mind, a thousand melodious bells should ring within your heart. Your whole body should thrill with joy. How can that be possible? If you have been starved for sugar for a long period of time and then someone reminds you of a delicious dessert, those nectarine bells will ring. The very mention of sugar will cause your mouth to water, delivering excitement and expectation. Why shouldn't the same be possible when remembering God?

Your mental associations with the Divine name should become so intense that each time the name is brought to your mind your whole body begins to resonate with that name. Thinking about God should be like thinking about someone who is supremely beloved—the essence of all beauty, joy, warmth, humor and acceptance.

This is the implication of this commandment. It does not mean, however, that you should stop repeating the name of God when your mind is clouded or your feelings are contracted. Rather, repeating the name at those times can be a most effective method of bringing the mind back to an elevated state. The commandment is intended to glorify the name of God and to encourage you to use it in any beneficial way.

ꬵourth Commandment

Remember the Sabbath Day to keep it holy.

Remember the Sabbath Day to keep it holy. Six days shalt thou labor and do all thy work, but the seventh day is the Sabbath of the Lord thy God. In it, thou shalt not do any work, nor thy son, nor thy daughter, nor thy manservant, nor thy maid servant, nor thy cattle nor the stranger that is within thy gates. For in six days, the Lord made heaven and earth, the sea, and all that is in them— and he rested on the seventh day; wherefore, the Lord blessed the Sabbath Day, and hallowed it. (KJV Exodus 20: 8—11)

The orthodox religious leaders of Christ's time were committed to a strict observance of this fourth commandment. However, their ritualistic concept was again and again challenged by Jesus as he continued to heal the sick even on the Sabbath day. One incident recounted in the New Testament tells how, on the Sabbath, Jesus healed a man who had been lame for a great many years:

Some time later, Jesus went up to Jerusalem for one of the Jewish festivals. Now there is in Jerusalem near the Sheep Gate a pool, which in Aramaic is called Bethesda and which is surrounded by five covered colonnades. Here a great number of disabled people used to lie—the blind, the lame, the paralyzed. One who was there had been an invalid for thirty-eight years. When Jesus saw him lying there and learned that he had been in this condition for a long time, he asked him, "Do you want to get well?"

"Sir," the invalid replied, "I have no one to help me into the pool when the water is stirred. While I am trying to get in, someone else goes down ahead of me." Then Jesus said to him, "Get up! Pick up your mat and walk." At once the man was cured; he picked up his mat and walked.

The day on which this took place was a Sabbath, and so the Jewish leaders said to the man who had been healed, "It is the Sabbath; the law forbids you to carry your mat." But he replied, "The man who made me well said to me, 'Pick up your mat and walk.' So they asked him, "Who is this fellow who told you to pick it up and walk?" The man who was healed had no idea who it was, for Jesus had slipped away into the crowd that was there. Later Jesus found him at the temple and said to him, "See, you are well again. Stop sinning or something worse may happen to you." The man went away and told the Jewish leaders that it was Jesus who had made him well.

So, because Jesus was doing these things on the Sabbath, the Jewish leaders began to persecute him. In his defense Jesus said to them, "My Father is always at his work to this very day, and I too am working."
(NIV John 5: 1-17)

This episode is suggestive of the necessity of outgrowing the ritualistic system of religion and its old traditions. Due to his illness, it was not possible for the man to follow the same rituals that the crowd had been following for years. Yet with the help of Christ, he was able to achieve the same goal.

Religious movement evolves rituals according to its need. When it is burdened by ritualistic rigidity, it degenerates into blind belief and superstition. A feeble mentality develops within when one follows a ritual robotically.

Jesus stated that the *"Sabbath was made for man, and not man for the Sabbath."* (KJV Mark 2: 27-28) All ritualistic aspects of religion must serve the cause of spiritual upliftment. If the Sabbath becomes a mere mechanical drudgery, the Sabbath must be outstepped by a heroic aspirant. Sustained by Christ Consciousness, an aspirant—like the lame man in the story—will no longer blindly depend on the "mat" of karmic conditions or society's rituals, but will transcend them and attain true spiritual freedom from all limitations in life.

As we reflect on this biblical episode, we realize that throughout human history many religious followers have chosen to honor a literal interpretation of this commandment and have respected a particular day of the week as a Sabbath, or a day of rest. Others have chosen to interpret the commandment more freely and define work and rest according to their own spiritual, personal, social and economic needs and goals.

However, even for those who have tried to adopt a literal Sabbath Day, activity never really ceases completely. They may abstain from certain forms of work, yet within their minds they may be calculating the money that they are accumulating in the bank, making plans for what must be done the next day when their job resumes, or judging those around them with swirling mental currents of attachment and hatred. Certainly this is not a Sabbath at all.

Similarly, within our bodies, activity never ceases. Imagine how much work goes on whenever we merely eat a small meal. The tongue, the teeth, the digestive organs and the circulatory system are ever busy. Thus, in all respects, it is impossible for human activity ever to cease. This being so, what then, is the real meaning of the Sabbath?

The Mystical Meaning of the Six Days of Creation and the Sabbath

According to Yogic philosophy, the six days of creation refer to God's projection of the universe in six planes. The first is the plane of Nature (*Prakriti*) or undifferentiated matter; the second is the plane of the Cosmic Mind (*Mahat*); the third is the plane of the ego principle (*Ahamkara Tattwa*); the fourth is the plane of the subtle elements; the fifth is the plane of the mind and senses; and the sixth is the plane of the physical body and the physical world. "Sabbath" refers to the transcendence of these six planes through the development of intuitive intellect and the experience of *samadhi*, or the state of superconsciousness that unfolds through meditation.

The six planes are also associated with the six centers in the *Sushumna*, the mystic channel associated with the spinal column in Kundalini Yoga. These centers are known as the *Swadhishthana, Muladhara, Manipura, Anahata, Vishuddhi,* and *Sahasrara Chakras.* When these six centers of the *Sushumna* and the six planes of the world are transcended, there arises a Sabbath—a complete termination of activity. Where activity exists, there is duality, and duality coexists with the planes of matter. When matter is transcended, one enjoys the absolute inactivity of the Spirit.

The effort to transcend the six planes, to transcend the world of duality, must be made by every spiritual aspirant. Keeping the Sabbath holy implies reflecting upon transcendence and attempting to practice it every day in whatever way possible.

Understanding Divine Transcendence

When Lord Jesus healed on the Sabbath rather than on an ordinary day, he was demonstrating the significance of viewing the Sabbath more on a level of consciousness than as a specific day of the week. It is more important to understand the profound mystical concept of Divine transcendence than to merely pursue the literal human concept of rest. The idea that God created the world, became exhausted and then rested is a projection of the human mind.

His rest is within Himself; rest is His very essential nature. God transcends creation.

In the Upanishads it is said that God created the whole world, permeates it, and yet at all times remains ten fingers above the world. He remains untouched. This is similar to a large Mack Truck passing through an archway with a clearance of ten fingers. There is a heavenly transcendental dimension within your consciousness wherein the whole world can be surpassed. Reaching out to that transcendental dimension within is the true observance of Sabbath.

Adoring God in Silence

The word "Sabbath" mystically signifies adoring God in silence. Every aspirant should set apart half an hour to an hour each day when he can retire into silent meditation. Similar to God retiring from His entire creation, you must retire from your entire creation—from your values, from your worries, from your concepts, from your notions. That retiring into the realm of spiritual silence is an important part of the practice of honoring the Sabbath and keeping it holy.

Discovering Inaction in Action

One of the major themes of the Bhagavad Gita is that it is possible to be dynamically active and yet possess a mind completely free from turmoil. When you have attained a transcendental level of consciousness, you rise above all normal concepts of activity and inactivity. You realize, "I am not this body that operates through the mind and senses. I am the Spirit, the nondual Self." Although as a personality you are involved in activity, deep within, you are not the "doer" or the "actor"—you are Spirit, beyond activity.

An enlightened Sage, free of egoistic desires, leaves the fruits of action in Divine Hands. Therefore, for a Sage, activity of the body does not affect the vision of inactivity of the Spirit. Though dynamically involved in activity, great Sages are completely inactive within. Similarly, with a higher level of awareness of your essential nature, you may continue to be busy and still keep the Sabbath holy. That is the true observance of Sabbath, the true transcendence of action.

Fifth Commandment

Honor thy father and thy mother.

In the Upanishads, it is said, *"Maitri devo bhava"*—"Let your mother be your God" and *"Pitri devo bhava"*—"Let your father be your God." In homes where there is an environment of love and warmth, it is easy for you to begin learning to honor and respect others through your primary relationship with your parents. It is easy to see God as the source of their wonderful care and affection. As you continue to mature, you begin to see God operating in your teachers and in all human relationships.

As long as you do not recognize God within other human beings, relationships remain shallow and fleeting, and there is no firm foundation supporting them. But when you begin to worship God through a relationship, you have discovered the great secret of experiencing true and enduring love.

As you become devoted to your elders and try to please them, you become more enduring, more patient. This allows you to grow up with discipline. On the other hand, in situations where children are constantly disrespectful to their elders and rebel against discipline, life begins on a shaky and discordant foundation.

Honoring your elders and seeing God within them is the first stage in a very important spiritual process that eventually culminates in the profound experience of Self-realization. When you attain this experience of Enlightenment, you realize God to be the essence or substratum of all that exists—of yourself as well as of all beings in this vast creation.

Can Parents Be Wrong?

In the lives of many people there are times when the commandment to honor one's parents cannot be followed strictly for practical or spiritual reasons.

Treading the spiritual path requires that an aspirant walk alone to a great extent and, in so doing, he cannot always harmonize with the wishes of his parents as much as the commandment would seem to imply.

Suppose your parents do not set a good moral example, or forbid you to enter into spiritual practices that would be meaningful to you. Should you, for their sake, destroy your mental peace and eventually become emotionally unstable, constantly giving them and those around you trouble? Or should you disobey their commands, integrate your personality and eventually become a delight to them?

Blind obedience to your parents is not good. Rather, honoring your parents implies possessing profound insight into the goal of life—God-realization—and how to attain it. If you are compelled by virtue to disagree with your parents, you must try not to offend them, but instead convince and persuade them that what you are doing is right. Human beings are not made of stone. Ultimately they may yield to the Truth. If you persist in showing them that the path you are treading is righteous and will eventually bring them much good, their resistance will crumble. They will soften and even begin to encourage your spiritual pursuits.

However, at times, despite one's best efforts to overcome parental opposition, some parents will just not be convinced. In that case, your movement towards righteousness is your first duty. Everything else becomes lesser.

Insight into this point is given in the accounts of the life of Saint Mira, a great lady Saint from the sixteenth century India. Mira was brought up in a royal family with an abundance of luxuries, but her heart was filled with devotion to Lord Krishna and a constant desire to worship him. At first, her husband, who was a very materialistic king, wanted to please Mira in every way. He built a temple for her and provided her with every convenience so that she could meditate. Gradually, however, the king found that his wife was more devoted to Krishna than to him, and he found that their relationship was no longer fulfilling. As a result, he began to hate her and plotted with other family members to destroy her.

As her relationship with her family became increasingly more painful, Mira wrote a letter to Tulsidas, a great Saint, asking his advice about her predicament. Tulsidas replied that ethical practices generally demand that there be harmony in the family and that one should obey one's parents and husband. However, advised the Sage, if those family members are against Krishna (God), then one must shun them as one would shun a great demon!

Ultimately, your dearest relative is God, and your movement to God is all that is truly essential in life. However, when "shunning" those who impede this movement, you ideally should make every effort to harmonize with others, without utilizing rough or condemning tactics, as you move patiently towards the goal of Self-realization.

Who Are Your Real Parents?

In the spiritual life of every human being, who really is your father, who really is your mother, and what is the purpose of this world? One's spiritual Father is God and one's Mother is *Prakriti*, or Nature, which sustains every soul. The world is a great family in which everything has been planned so that the soul will gradually become educated and unfold its potentialities. In this process of following a spiritual life, these Divine parents must be honored and obeyed at all costs.

Obedience to God and Nature implies that one has a deep sensitivity to life and its demands. The voice of God, the Father, speaks to you through your conscience, through your purified intellect. Mother Nature, or *Prakriti*, benevolently changes your conditions and circumstances, as well as your body, mind and senses, so that you can evolve in the best manner possible.

Through prosperity and adversity, the Divine Hands of your Father and Mother—God and Nature—are guiding your soul to Enlightenment. Developing profound faith in that Divine Plan, in the Divine order that permeates your life, is the real meaning of "honoring thy father and thy mother." It should be kept in view that in the final attainment, God and Nature (*Prakriti*) are One and the same.

Sixth Commandment

Thou shalt not kill.

The sixth commandment—*Thou shalt not kill*—is generally interpreted as an injunction against murdering other human beings. But, more than restraining one from a particular type of violent action, the commandment is actually rooted in a deeper, more abstract understanding of the entire concept of *ahimsa*, or nonviolence.

Because a human being represents a very advanced level of consciousness, killing another person is most cruel and corrupt. No happiness or harmony can be acquired through killing. Any happiness acquired through bloodshed will eventually devour the killers like a tiger devouring its victims.

Ideally, killing should not be promoted in any way, neither by individuals, nor by the politicians of a nation. There is no abiding righteousness or goodness in killing. However, realizing that ideal requires raising public morality to a level where people recognize the vanity of war as well as the complete uselessness of killing those who are labeled as enemies in the name of political balance and harmony.

Most people in the world consider *Thou shalt not kill* as a commandment against the killing of human beings, but society does not think that this should apply to the killing of animals. From a more advanced spiritual perspective, however, the ideal of nonviolence extends to the killing of animals as well—particularly in those situations in which human survival does not depend upon the consumption of animals.

Insight into Nonviolence

There are an infinite number of situations in which people hurt one another, intentionally or unintentionally. Therefore, a true understanding of nonviolence requires deep reflection and great philosophical insight. Sometimes we hurt others as an expression of ill-conceived righteousness. Suppose, for example, that we want someone to do something that we consider to be right, so we raise a whip to force the person to do it. And sometimes when a person has done something wrong, we adopt the practice of punishment. Adopting cruelty to teach and punish others is the law of the masses, but it should not be the law of aspirants. As an aspirant, it is possible to see things from a higher perspective. Understand that what seems hateful or crude in another's personality is actually the Divine Self lulled into inertia or sleep. Your task is to adore God, no matter how much God may be sleeping within that individual. Such adoration requires patience and endurance. Those who appear to behave in a hateful way have within them the same potentiality, the same sweetness of the Self that you have. It is by awakening their minds to the perception of their own potentiality that you will most effectively help them conquer the defects of their personality.

Crudeness should never be answered with crudeness. Cruelty can never be corrected by cruelty. The goal in virtuous human relations is to awaken others, not to crush them. Strive to influence others by virtue, not by hatred; melt the hearts of others by your righteousness, not by proving that you can match or even surpass their maliciousness.

When you force another person to do as you want, there is no fulfillment in his heart. There is only agony and insecurity. Unfortunately, thousands of families and businesses maintain "harmony" at home or at work through threats that generate fear. But there is no real virtue that arises due to such methods. When you terrify another person into a state of passive virtue, you are treating him as if he were a circus lion. In the circus, bloodthirsty lions are kept as meek as sheep under the power of the electrical whip. However, their meekness is not authentic.

Understand that every evil situation that you encounter is a challenge to awaken your faith in virtue. Every negative circumstance in the world is daring you to assert righteousness and see to what extent you can be triumphant.

For it is in the celebration of the positive that there is fulfillment in life. There is nothing as thrilling as melting the heart of a cruel person with goodness and seeing him become a compassionate and virtuous person. Such a genuine transformation could not result from your being harsh or cruel.

Tapping into the Source of the Infinite Power Within

Violence is a method of compulsion arising from a weak, fearful and impatient mind. Nonviolence is an expression of a highly integrated personality that arises from a strong, perceptive mind. To cultivate nonviolence within your own heart, learn to search deep within to discover the roots of mental agitation and fear that result from faultfinding judgments against yourself and others. If the debilitating hatred you feel for another person could be transformed and transcended, imagine how much energy you would have! Imagine what could be accomplished if you refused to waste any more energy on directing anger and hatred towards another! Such is the challenge before every spiritual aspirant.

There is an infinite source of power within each person. We need only to tap into it by removing the obstructions created by the mind. Through reflection and self-introspection, the causes of the obstructions reveal themselves. It is then that we can persistently remove them from the very depths of the unconscious.

Strength of mind lies not in how much you can intimidate others, but in how well you can control your own agitation and anger through reflection, sublimation and finally transcendence of these traits. In provocative conditions, can you restrain anger that dissipates your energy? Can you avoid reciprocating, and as a result, express endurance, patience, and eventually profound love towards a person who is trying to provoke you?

If so, your mind will be filled with the radiant rays of spiritual peace that exist in the very depths of your being. It will be filled with a sublimating force that is so powerful that a violent person approaching you with an evil intention may suddenly forget all about it! And gradually it will exert a transforming influence on the person who was compelled to express his violence.

It is said that once several royal princes decided that Buddha was not an authentic teacher, and they wanted to ridicule him to test his patience. With that desire in mind, they gathered together, mounted their horses, and galloped into Buddha's abode.

When they entered, however, they found everything so peaceful and serene around them that they and even their horses began to relax. They were so awed by the influence of Buddha's presence that they discarded their evil intent, bowed down before him and requested that they be initiated into his order.

This story illustrates the power that nonviolence exerts over others. If you become aware of that power within another person, as the princes did with Buddha, the tendency to vent even the slightest anger or hate will evaporate. You recognize the exalted and authentic love that radiates not only from that person, but also from deep within your own heart. It is a wealth beyond measure.

Seventh Commandment

Thou shalt not commit adultery.

The seventh commandment—*Thou shalt not commit adultery*—must be studied with a mature and objective mind. A corresponding virtue of great importance in the Yogic tradition, intrinsically related to fidelity, is known in Sanskrit as *brahmacharya*.

What Is Brahmacharya?

Brahmacharya, in its most restricted definition, implies control and sublimation of sex energy through the practice of celibacy and restraint of sex pleasures. Generally, therefore, people think of a *brahmachari* as a young person or a monk who is celibate and unmarried. However, the term has profound implications. In the deeper philosophical sense, *brahmacharya* implies the control and sublimation of biological passion, leading to the realization of a far more exalted state of Bliss. This inspiring and elevating love unites not just the sexes, but unites every individual with the universe and with all that exists. The ideal of *brahmacharya* asserts that a human being, whether male or female, is intrinsically the Self (*Brahman*). Thus, their instinct to love must ultimately be completely and sublimely fulfilled in the state of Self-realization, wherein union with God, the Self-in-all, is attained.

Therefore, in ancient India, for the purpose of raising the consciousness of humanity to this exalted state, Sages divided the human lifetime into four twenty-five year stages or *ashrams*. According to this system, people are to spend the first twenty-five years of their life in the *brahmacharya ashram*, or student life. The second twenty-five years are devoted to the *grihastha ashram* or householder/married life. The third stage is *vanaprastha ashram*, the retired stage, focused upon the practice of austerity and the dissemination of wisdom in forest schools. The fourth and final stage is *sanyasa ashram* or renunciation.

This ancient system of the *brahmacharya* ashram was designed for students who were below the age of twenty-five to devote their time and energy to intensive spiritual studies under the guidance of a Guru or spiritual teacher. To elevate this educational experience of contemplation and reflection, they were instructed to remain celibate until the householder phase of their life. The ideal of this discipline encouraged young people to redirect this powerful energy inward, toward reaching higher states of spiritual consciousness, while preventing them from being caught up in the frivolities and problems that can result due to overindulgence and misuse of sex.

Whether a person is married or unmarried, the biological demand of life, the instinctive urge for procreation and passion continues to assert itself. It influences all people, young and old, in all stages of life. A complete mastery over this vital and powerful energy requires the same profound understanding necessary for conquering the subtle and potent roots of violence in the human personality. Therefore, *brahmacharya*, in a broader sense, is to be understood and practiced by people at all stages of life, whether they are single or a householder.

Mere externals are not an indication of one's advancement in *brahmacharya*. An unmarried person can be more preoccupied with sexuality than one who is a householder and may have many thoughts and fantasies about passion swirling around within his mind. A married couple with children, on the other hand, may reach a level of understanding in which they realize that sex is not an end in itself. They may learn to fulfill many of their sentiments and feelings by honoring God within each other and within themselves on deeper levels, no longer placing so much emphasis on sex. In that case, their relationship becomes far more profound, sustained by a greater understanding of true *brahmacharya*.

The Human Need for Love and Creative Fulfillment

This compellingly powerful and inherent urge that operates within every human being to create and to commune with all that exists is the essential yearning of every soul, although most people are not consciously aware of it. The more familiar manifestation of this longing is the instinctive, biological impulse to reproduce and to become involved in a passionate relationship. This aspect begins to open the heart center and can give one the experience of connecting deeply with another individual. This relationship of love, however, is merely a shadow of the ecstasy that is experienced when your soul communes with all that exists. That motivation for inner creativity and expansion of the soul begins to reach its ultimate fulfillment when one becomes more spiritually evolved and possesses a highly intuitive intellect.

Until one is evolved enough to experience true Cosmic Consciousness and Divine Love, one needs interpersonal relationships and family involvements to help awaken the desire for this lofty form of love. A human being must be creatively fulfilled. If you do not experience a deeper form of inspiration on the higher mental and spiritual levels, then you begin to explore the creative urges on the physical and instinctual planes. Nature continues to awaken within you the idea of loving the Self—a love that can be difficult to understand—by manifesting the more easily understood varieties of love in the world: passionate love, parental love, love between friends, love between a teacher and a student, etc.

If one becomes captured by the illusion of physical pleasure, it is possible to forget that you are not merely a biological personality. You are a human being with the possibility of transcending biological instincts and enjoying the Bliss of intuitive understanding. When the mental energy traveling through the senses is redirected by intuitive understanding, your thoughts become clear and your mind develops sensitivity to the deeper harmony inherent in all that is. You now delight in a far more profound joy in life.

The moment spiritual advancement enables you to begin to enjoy intuitive expansion, you discover the majesty of consciousness and the ingenuity of the soul. The moment that vision arises, you graduate beyond the need for biological creativity. When you compare the mind in these two states, you begin to understand the sweetness and grandeur that arise due to mental expansion. This higher form of joy permeates the mind and heart of the individual. As a result, the inclination towards sexual pleasures is automatically fulfilled by the genuine sublimity of exalted consciousness. This is what is referred to as sex-sublimation or *brahmacharya* in Yogic terminology.

Fidelity and the Purpose of Marriage

Fidelity is not as simple as just being married and abstaining from sexual relations with anyone other than your spouse. A couple may stay together without any outward infidelity, yet, since a higher love has not dawned, they will always feel insecure about their relationship. Their love is simply a matter of attachment and entanglement, and in most cases, will eventually fade. Fidelity, then, is not merely external in a relationship. It implies that those who love one another are faithful to each other within their souls. It implies that they strive to serve God within their partner and to acquire a profoundly mature understanding of what love really is.

One who practices *brahmacharya* understands that any genuine loving relationship cannot continue to exist if its sole purpose is pleasure. Love between partners is fraudulent if it depends entirely upon a passionate confirmation of their love and has not engendered mutual respect and Divine Love for God within each other. If you make sexual pleasure predominant in a marriage, then you are overlooking the central spiritual goal of marriage and are practicing a subtle but significant form of infidelity as well.

Seeking pleasure does not refer only to sexual delight in this context. It refers to the mind's infatuation with all objects that are loved and to any egoistic delight that the relationship can provide. This also applies to the love between a child and his parents, between friends, and to all forms of love that exist in human life. None of these loving relationships should be considered solely as a means to a selfish end. Rather, they should become a means of elevation, upliftment and inspiration for both parties. Your love for another passes the Divine test if you and the one you love are both led to a higher spiritual summit through your love. But if your love degrades you or your loved one in any way, there is a lack of true *brahmacharya*, a lack of true fidelity.

A Philosophical Look at Sexual Differences

Men and women essentially are sexless. They are spirits—not males or females. In the plane of spirit there are no sexes. However, in the process of spiritual evolution, it is necessary for the soul to discover certain qualities of the mind and heart. That need polarizes itself into the form of male and female personalities. In the course of the soul's repeated incarnations, females have not been females in each lifetime, and males have not always been males. Their souls have assumed different personalities—a male in some lifetimes and a female in other incarnations.

The mind, with its need for the fulfillment of both reason and emotion, evolved the physical body. When the need for emotion is highlighted in a particular embodiment, the spirit chooses to operate through a female personality. When the need for reason is emphasized, a male personality manifests. This, however, is from a generalized point of view. There are many exceptions to this rule.

Depending upon how they identify with their biological structures as well as their sexual identity, males and females consider themselves to be imperfect and incomplete without another. Drawn by a powerful magnetic force that they do not understand, they begin to relate to each other in diverse ways. If that force is properly understood, it will lead to the practice of *brahmacharya,* and a higher form of relationship will begin to unfold. If that force is not properly understood, one is simply captured by the instinctive demands for biological procreation and passion.

Although you may be drawn to a partner by instinctive and karmic factors, gradually you will come to realize that the purpose of love and married life is not merely to derive comfort and pleasure. Rather, partners in a healthy and meaningful love relationship learn to expand their heart center, sublimate their selfish demands for pleasure, and become endowed with increasing magnanimity, inspiration, patience, self-sacrifice and understanding. If they are able to accomplish this, they are promoting a mutual, spiritual upliftment towards higher levels of inner joy, and their union will be fulfilling. If they do not, then their union is simply an external show and will not lead to any real satisfaction.

The Influence of Brahmacharya on Society

The ideal of *brahmacharya* does not regard sex as shameful or sinful, but considers it as a highly creative force that should be respected. The ideal of *brahmacharya* requires that your mind understands the implications and purpose of sex in your life. Sex can be a means to a more profound and deeper love if that energy is utilized towards spiritual upliftment. However, if a deeper love is not kept in view, then sexual relations become debilitating and degrading.

The misuse of sex implies a lack of *brahmacharya*. When sex is misused it can result in all types of vices and criminality. If a person is overwhelmed with sexual desires and those desires are not fulfilled, the mind can be influenced by tremendous restlessness that gives rise to egoism, pride, jealousy, abnormal greed, violence and many other negative qualities in the human personality.

Parents lacking *brahmacharya* will have little understanding of their responsibilities and the true meaning of love. As a result, they sacrifice each other as well as their children in their mad chase for what seems to be pleasurable and delightful. Children that grow up in a family that is not pervaded by a spirit of *brahmacharya* often become psychologically ill, because they have not been influenced by higher ideals. They live in a chaotic environment of delusion, fraud and deception that has a profound impact on their lives. On the other hand, children brought up by parents who are infused with the spirit of *brahmacharya* generally are a blessing to themselves and to society.

In a society that places so much emphasis on sex and physical beauty, it is difficult for a person to age with any dignity. One may follow a path of passion as a young person and feel quite delighted with such a life. However, in later years as one ages and beauty fades, without the person having developed an inner spiritual life, the mind can sink into gloom and darkness. Lacking the same youthful appearance and passion one had in youth, the aging person can feel like a useless failure.

Rather than reaping a harvest of wisdom from a life well lived, many elderly people feel ridiculed by the younger generation and are obsessed with trying to recapture their youthful charms. Society has taught them only to worship the spring of their life and therefore they do not see the value of their inner spiritual identity. This situation is terribly degrading for a society.

However, the spirit of *brahmacharya* helps to promote a culture in which people can age with grace and feel a profound sense of being appreciated. In a truly healthy society, elderly people should be revered for their wisdom and experience and their ideas should be a source of delight for all. The notion that memory must fail and brain cells must degenerate as one grows older does not hold true for those who live a profoundly spiritual life. They become more capable of advanced thought and creative understanding.

Converting Passion into a Spiritual Force

Sublimated sex energy—known in Yogic terminology as *ojas shakti*—produces an extraordinary vitality in the human body and mind. A mind that vibrates with spiritual strength radiates effulgence that gives a glow and luster to the entire personality. That magnetic effulgence has a powerful effect on others and helps them to perceive their own potential strength in a most inspiring and Divine way.

The welfare of the world depends greatly upon how the human mind learns to convert its passions into spiritual force. Political and social ideals are wonderful, but they cannot be practiced with much success unless human minds possess greater strength and depth of understanding. This is why Mahatma Gandhi asserted the importance of the virtues of truth, nonviolence and *brahmacharya*, and encouraged the practice of these virtues on an international level. He wanted those who followed him to adopt these virtues to the best of their capacity.

When the human mind is constantly afflicted by anger, passion and the distraction of worldly acquisitions, it becomes insensitive to its deeper possibilities. Under their influence, life becomes a frantic pursuit of wealth and pleasures of the senses that can never provide an authentic or lasting fulfillment. Therefore, even while one is young and energetic, it is important to strive to lift oneself above these burdensome traits by understanding and practicing the ideals of *brahmacharya*, truth and nonviolence. Inspired by these ideals, one can discover the great joy that unfolds within the human heart through love of the Self—the essence of all that is lovable.

What Is Real Love?

Real love is neither passionate, nor fatherly, nor motherly, nor friendly. It is far more profound. In one of the Upanishads, great Sage Yajnavalkya teaches his wife Maitreyi: *"Atmanastu kamaya sarvam priyam bhavati"*—"For the sake of the Self, all becomes dear." What you are actually attempting to love, through your loving sentiments and feelings, is the Self. That Self is the basis of the entire universe. Essentially, it is that Self that everyone yearns to love, because the Self is the ultimate fulfillment of love. One actually perceives the Self in all people and objects, and for this reason these become the focus of love. However, when the Self no longer seems to reflect within them, they become meaningless to a person.

Brahmacharya, properly understood, binds one human being to another through an exploration of the deeper planes of feelings that exist within the human heart. It is in those planes where God abides. All human beings are merely symbols of that Divinity. It is only when profound love of God arises that you can truly love other human beings.

Love cannot be confined to your family or to a few friends. It becomes universal, Cosmic, without a shadow of sentimentality of a lower nature, without a shadow of enslavement to biological instinct or passion. This is the indescribably dynamic love that exists in the heart of Christ, in the heart of Buddha, in the hearts of all Sages and Saints whose love continues to shine as a source of eternal light and power for all.

Eighth Commandment

Thou shalt not steal.

The eighth commandment—*Thou shalt not steal*—addresses a human vice that assumes numerous forms of expression, both gross and subtle, and has many psychological implications. In Raja Yoga, *asteya*, or nonstealing, is one of the five great *yamas* or ethical restraints. *Asteya* implies freedom from desiring, misappropriating or stealing the possessions of others.

The Psychological Basis of Stealing

The urge to steal results from the illusory belief that happiness comes from objects. Afflicted with this deception, one can be overwhelmed by the urge to take things that seem to be giving happiness to others. It is a blend of greed, selfishness, and lack of control over the senses.

A thief steals because he feels that he cannot be happy without the objects he craves and his mind lacks the patience to earn these things in a righteous way. His mind may at first think, "You can acquire those things by working for them." But eventually his mind changes its perspective and says, "Why should I? Why not just enter into a crowd and pick a pocket or two! Or I can just sneak into a house, showing a gun and a masked face, and get what I want. Who is going to catch me?"

The greedy mind is not aware of the darker implications of what that action will do to him or others. It does not perceive the pain it will inflict, or what the person will feel if they lose things that they have loved or righteously earned by hard work. Due to intense selfishness, the mind behaves like a depraved vulture and promotes indulgence in falsehood.

The Many Forms of Stealing

Stealing does not simply imply breaking into someone's house or business and physically taking something that does not belong to you. Every ethical person knows that overt stealing is immoral and degrading to a human being and should not be done. However, there are subtler forms of theft that many people never reflect upon.

If you develop jealousy towards the prosperity of others and feel that their happiness should have been yours—that is a subtle form of psychological stealing. If you obstruct someone's progress, or interfere with his opportunities, or redirect money towards yourself that should have been his in order to become wealthier or more prosperous yourself—that is stealing. If you go out of your way to harm others for revenge—you are a thief. If you misappropriate others' possessions by adopting any immoral or illegal methods—that is stealing. When you involve yourself in any criminal activity—you are stealing. In all criminal acts you are acquiring, misappropriating, or somehow altering something that is not rightfully yours.

If a lawyer takes up a case knowing that the person has committed a crime and he helps the person acquire freedom—he is stealing. If a doctor tells a person who doesn't need an operation that he needs one, just for the sake of money—he is stealing. Whenever a person in any occupation has no sense of serving humanity, but only thinks about his own benefit or acquisition of money—that is stealing. Writers steal from others and claim authorship of works they have not written. Businessmen steal ideas, inventions and strategies from each other. Stealing goes on in every field of endeavor among people who feel they must compete for success.

Even in spiritual matters there are many subtle forms of stealing. For example, if a person constantly quotes from great men or copies their external behavior or appearance, but makes no effort to understand and assimilate the real meaning of their teachings into his own life—he is a kind of spiritual thief.

Speaking from a more advanced, philosophical point of view, it is also a form of stealing even to consider your physical body to be your own: "This is mine, and this is me." The body doesn't belong to you (the ego self); it belongs to a Divine Plan, it belongs to God. Any form of egoistic assertion of "I-ness" and "mine-ness" is a form of stealing. The Gita states that you are a thief if you enjoy objects of the world for the sake of your ego without remembering God, without invoking God in your pleasures, without recognizing that it is actually God, not the objects, Who is the source of joy. You are stealing things that do not belong to you.

Thus, as you advance on the spiritual path, you begin to practice a higher level of *asteya*. You no longer consider even your body or limited personality to be your own. When you have understood this Truth in the depths of your being, you have attained the highest form of perfection in *asteya*.

What Is True Prosperity?

It is only due to ignorance that you feel that an object will give you happiness. Objects that belong to others cannot really give them permanent happiness, any more than they can give you perpetual happiness. The idea, "I will become happy if I have that," is a falsehood. Greed is a modification of that indulgence in falsehood. Since you are unable to understand that happiness does not dwell within objects, you develop the greedy desire: "May I have more and more."

A rich man, whose millions multiply his worries a millionfold is not really prosperous. His mental energy is dissipated because he constantly thinks about how he can increase his fortune and become wealthier. He may be so greedy that he lacks even the contentment of any ordinary man.

Although you may have a lot of money in the bank and you may be the legal owner of a vast amount of property or a big business, you may not enjoy true prosperity psychologically or spiritually. If all your prosperity is in possessions, in lawyers and in property deeds—but not in your own heart, then you are truly not prosperous. When you are greedy, your will becomes weak. As a result of this weakness, you are not able to obtain the very objects that you greedily desire. Or if you do acquire them, they will become a source of pain.

There is a strange law operating in the Divine Plan: If you do not deserve an object that you desire, that object will reject you. Even if you succeed in possessing it, the object will be painful because it will create mental complexes. When you acquire wealth out of greed, that wealth creates fear because you will always be afraid of losing it. Further, you may want to assert that you are wealthy, and as a result you will become conceited, arrogant, and insensitive, preventing you from enjoying inner peace. Therefore, you will not really be able to enjoy your prosperity. As a result, prosperity becomes more of a curse than a boon.

An interesting parable is told about Goddess Lakshmi, the Goddess of Prosperity: A devotee was practicing meditation and had a strange vision when he invoked the presence of Lakshmi Devi. The Goddess, whom he expected to appear before him in a luminous and radiant form, manifested with her forehead and feet badly bruised. Seeing Lakshmi Devi in this strange condition, the devotee asked, "Oh Goddess, how is this possible? How can you, who are the giver of prosperity to all, have such terrible bruises?"

The Goddess replied, "Oh devotee, I will explain to you. There are so many worldly-minded people who pursue me, and yet do not deserve me. And I have to go on kicking them from morning until night. Imagine how much my feet hurt because I must go on doing that day after day! And then there are some rare souls who tread the path of spirituality and are so dispassionate that they don't want me at all. In the Divine plan, however, they must have some of my wealth in order to help mankind. So I go to their doors and, adopting the Eastern method, repeatedly bow and strike my head against their thresholds to persuade them to accept my prosperity. Since this goes on day by day, my forehead has become terribly bruised!"

The parable shows that if you are devoid of greed, you attract the Goddess of Prosperity, who wants to bestow her blessings. On the other hand, if you pursue objects through greed, then the Goddess of Prosperity continues kicking you, as it were.

If you are established in virtue, you will do what is needed to deserve your desired prosperity and the appropriate fruit of your efforts will be drawn to you spontaneously. If you perform your self-effort in the world without being greedy, everything that you need in your spiritual evolution will manifest automatically. In a mysterious way, Nature will give you what you require, and you will be able to use your prosperity well. Thus, the practice of *asteya* opens your heart to the abundance of Divine Consciousness and leads you to the treasure of treasures—Self-realization!

Ninth Commandment

Thou shalt not bear false witness.

The ninth commandment—*Thou shalt not bear false witness*—is profoundly related to *satyam* (truthfulness) and is one of the basic *yamas*, or restraints, in Raja Yoga. All Sages and Saints have emphasized the need for practicing truth and have considered this to be the foundation for spiritual movement. To be able to profoundly practice truthfulness on all levels of your personality, your intellect must comprehend what the truth is. If your intellect is unable to comprehend the truth, then you cannot live by it.

Truth, in fact, is God Himself. In this world of illusion, the only Truth is *Brahman*, the Absolute Self. The highest practice of truth implies moving towards *Brahman* and attaining Self-realization. In actuality, untruth has no existence. However, the intellect is dominated by many shadows of falsehood, and these shadows go to form the realities of the world-process. You may nurture the thought that you will become truly happy due to a particular development or because of a relationship with a particular person. Although this may appear to be true for a time, ultimately, this is not truth. However, most human values are sustained by those shadows of falsehood, and many times the mind becomes so submerged in its glue that one cannot even bear listening to the slightest glimmer of truth.

How to Practice Truthfulness

From a relative point of view, truth is practiced on three levels of your personality: thoughts, words, and actions. The thoughts that you entertain within your mind, the words that you speak, and the actions that you perform must all be in harmony with your spiritual movement leading to Self-realization.

Truth on the Level of Thoughts

You are practicing truth on the mental level when you study scriptures under proper guidance and, thereby, allow your mind to be sensitive to the higher values and meaning of life. If the mind is burdened by egoistic desires and crowded by impressions of anger and hate, your intellect will not be able to grasp the nature of truth.

If you are truthful at the level of your mind, then automatically your words and actions will be true. However, such mental purity is an advanced attainment. Therefore, the initial focus for a spiritual aspirant is practicing truth at the level of speech and actions.

Truth on the Level of Speech

For most people, the practice of truthfulness at the verbal level implies speaking about things as they seem to be, in a clear and factual way, without any distortion, modification, or concealment. However, according to Yoga, speaking the truth is not quite that simple.

Consider the situation in which a person speaks the truth with the negative intention of hurting someone else. Suppose, for example, that you have a business competitor that you would like to eliminate. One day you see him doing something that others would consider erroneous, and you decide to expose this to the public to ruin his business image. You wait for the occasion when there is an appreciable gathering of people and then come forward to say, "I am the practitioner of truth. I will tell you exactly what I have seen this man do!"

You have spoken the truth, no doubt, but your truth violated the basic ethical principle of *ahimsa* or nonviolence. Your intention was directed more towards hurting the person for your own advantage than promoting the truth. If your speech is compelled by anger or hate and is intended to harm someone, then although technically your words are perfectly truthful, from a spiritual point of view, it is not truth. Your "truth" is a form of falsehood. You are actually perpetuating your ego, which is false, rather than serving truth.

One of the most well known illustrations of the misuse of truth on the verbal level is the story in the Mahabharata of how Draupadi, the wife of the Pandavas, insulted the Kaurava leader, Duryodhana, with harsh words that accelerated the beginning of the Mahabharata War. As recounted in this great epic work, the five Pandavas and their wife Draupadi were living in a royal palace that had been designed in a most unique way; it was constructed of transparent walls and floors that shimmered like pools of water.

One day, their enemy, Duryodhana, walked into the palace to observe its unusual architecture. Disoriented by the transparent walls, he banged against the walls because he couldn't see where he was going. Perplexed by the optical illusion of the shimmering floors, he lifted his clothes as if preparing to walk through pools of water. These and similar actions of Duryodhana were observed by Draupadi, who then laughed at him and cried out, "Behold, the son of a blind king!"

These words of Draupadi were perfectly truthful in a factual sense. Duryodhana was indeed the son of King Dhritarashtra, who had been born blind. Nevertheless, the words were spoken to injure the feelings of Duryodhana, and they caused great animosity. In the course of time, Duryodhana's desire to avenge these words of ridicule was one of the main causes of the Mahabharata War.

Thus, one must understand that in speaking the truth, one's intention is more important than mere factual observation. The great gift of speech is a powerful tool of your personality. It should not be misused due to egoistic aberrations. The "truth" you convey to another person can encourage or discourage him. If you disparage a person by your words, then you have not understood the importance of being artistic in your speech, and you are not practicing truth on the verbal level.

Being artistic with your speech requires maturity and deep insight and is a reflection of great spiritual advancement. There is a saying in Sanskrit: *"Satyam vada, priyam vada"*—"Speak the truth, but only that truth that is pleasant." Be careful: If your truth is twisting your tongue, don't speak; if your truth is going to create bitterness, keep quiet. In those situations, it is better and more truthful to remain silent.

One must learn the art of expressing even a bitter truth in a pleasant manner. It is possible to point out someone's mistakes in such a manner that the person recognizes his errors and feels inspired to change. If you point out a person's mistake with sincerity and gentleness, he becomes appreciative of your concern and compassion. On the other hand, you can point out a person's mistakes in an insulting manner that causes the person to be an object of ridicule. As a result, he develops animosity and the mistake is never corrected.

That is why great Sages and Saints are loved by all, despite the fact that they may call out to people, "You dull wits, I am speaking to you, and you do not hear. Wake up!" The words of a Sage are spoken with such profound intrinsic compassion and nonviolence that no one objects to hearing them; rather, they celebrate their words of truth again and again.

Truth on the Level of Action

The third aspect of the practice of truthfulness involves performing actions that are in harmony with your convictions, actions that promote harmony in others. If actions are performed on that basis, you are practicing truthfulness in an effective manner.

While practicing truth, you may have to take recourse to words that appear to be lies and actions that seem deceptive. Great men of all ages have had to use insight into human psychology in order to promote truth.

Buddha once told his disciples a parable about a fire that was rapidly spreading in a great hall. The hall contained many children, but because the children had been enclosed in an area surrounded by walls, they were unaware of the fire and the danger to their lives. Concerned for their safety, the owner of the hall rushed in with a plan to get the children out of the building quickly, without causing them to be alarmed. He told them, "Come with me and I will give you toys. I have wonderful toy horses and elephants and animals of all types." Enchanted, the children all rushed to follow him as he left the burning hall. In promising to give the toys, the man's intention was to get the children out before they were injured or killed in the fire. Although he lied about why the children were leaving the building, his intention was to promote a greater truth.

Similarly, in dealing with different personalities and situations, one's intentions are really more important than simple facts. If any action serves the purpose of helping people to prevail over their shortcomings or to remedy their troubles, then that action is truthful.

A person who practices truth must honor his word. If you have promised something that is righteous, fulfill your promise. However, if you have promised something that will hurt another person, it is better to break that type of promise. Being punctual and observing time also promotes the practice of truthfulness. Time is of great importance in all dealings with human beings. If you tell a person to meet you at a particular time, but you show up an hour late, that's practicing falsehood.

Thus, keeping your promises to others, punctuality, sincerity, and humility are all expressions of the practice of truth on an everyday level. All these help lead you to the advanced practice of Truth, allowing your mind to flow towards the highest Truth—God.

The Power of Truthfulness

Since the practice of *satyam* implies an all-sided integration of personality based upon the vision of truth, it becomes a source of tremendous spiritual power. Raja Yoga Sutras states: *"Satya Pratishthaayaam Kriyaa-phalaashrayattwam."*— "By being established in truthfulness, a Yogi acquires the power of achieving the fruit of whatever action he performs." This implies that when a Sage utters a word, that word will not go in vain. The projects he adopts will not fail.

On a more profound level, this statement points to the fact that as you become increasingly perfected in your perception of truth, your personality becomes so integrated that you are in complete harmony with the Cosmic Will. Thus, the very thoughts that arise within your mind will carry the Divine authority of the Cosmic Mind. When a Sage is in tune with the Cosmic Mind, his thoughts reflect Cosmic thought and the intentions that operate through his mind are Cosmic intentions.

The Upanishads state, *"Satyamevajayate naanritam"*—"If you are practicing truth, the victory is yours." Although truth may not triumph easily, if you hold firmly to the ideal of the truth that you have glimpsed, you will eventually see that truth triumph over all obstacles. Ultimately, you will attain the Absolute Truth—Self-realization.

Tenth Commandment

Thou shalt not covet.

This commandment enjoins the practice of *aparigraha* (noncovetousness), the last of the *yamas* or ethical restraints of Raja Yoga. In Yoga philosophy, *asteya* and *aparigraha*—nonstealing and noncovetousness—are closely related sister virtues that are both directed towards the removal of greed.

If a person is dominated by a highly intense and perverted form of greed, he chooses the path of *steya*, or stealing. He waits until someone acquires an interesting object and then plots to grab that object from him, directly or indirectly, adopting methods that are unrighteous.

On the other hand, if the greed is more moderate, a person tends toward *parigraha* (covetousness). Adopting methods that are normally considered righteous, he continues to crave objects and accumulates more and more of them, hoarding them beyond his needs. Neither has the person stolen from others, nor has he misappropriated what they already possess. But he simply is obsessed with the idea, "If I have more and more, I will be happy."

The Burden of Covetousness

Afflicted by covetousness, you strive incessantly to multiply your possessions. Instead of having two pairs of shoes, you have fifty pairs; instead of having a few sweaters, you have a hundred sweaters! As a result, all year long you have to watch over your things to see that they don't get mildewed or moth-eaten. Afraid to lose all the possessions that you have acquired, you become tied to a place, tied to objects. You are a constant caretaker of things that you are not going to use—things that simply become a source of an endless headache for you. Furthermore, there is a great illusion involved in the idea that by acquiring more and more possessions you will become secure and comfortable. It is like chasing a mirage in order to quench your thirst.

If you were to study your life and the lives of people around you, you would realize that "more" doesn't necessarily mean "happier." A person who is poor thinks that if only he had sufficient money, he would be happy. But the moment he becomes more prosperous, he wants to have more and more and never feels contented. Normally, as wealth increases, discontent increases in direct proportion, unless you have developed spiritual insight. A simple parable is told that illustrates this point.

The Entanglement of "99"

There was once a blacksmith who enjoyed his work immensely, and although he labored very hard, he continued singing joyfully as he worked. When his wealthy neighbor heard him singing, he became extremely jealous. "How can it be," the neighbor thought to himself, "that with all my wealth, I can't even sleep due to worries and anxiety, and yet my blacksmith neighbor, who is less fortunate, is always so happy? Though he works very hard, hammering iron sheets close to a hot fire, he enjoys his life and his work!" Unable to bear this situation a moment longer, the jealous neighbor thought and thought, and then came up with a simple plan.

Putting his scheme into effect, the wealthy neighbor secretly threw a bag containing ninety-nine dollars into the shop of the blacksmith. When the blacksmith entered his shop, he found the bag and wondered how it had gotten there. Unable to solve the mystery, he decided to keep the money and make good use of it.

The idea then came to his mind, "It is only one dollar less than a hundred. It would have been better if it was a hundred—a nice, even number." So the next day he worked very hard and, instead of just earning one dollar, he brought his total to one-hundred-twenty-four. Then he thought, "If the amount I had was just one dollar more, it would be a perfect mathematical amount." So the next day he worked hard again, and the pattern continued— always needing a little more to make a nice, round figure. As the days passed, the blacksmith lost the mental peace he had always enjoyed in his work and he stopped singing. Of course, the wealthy neighbor was delighted, because his plan had worked, just as he had hoped!

One day the blacksmith suddenly realized that he was becoming sick, weak and restless. Then he reflected, "All my trouble started from those ninety-nine dollars." He gathered that money and now realizing it came from his wealthy neighbor, threw the money back over the fence into the rich man's yard, thinking that he could surely make good use of it.

In the Hindi language, there is a proverb that was inspired by this story: "Do not be entangled by ninety-nine." The moment you are caught by the illusion of needing a certain amount of money to be happy, you become entangled, like the blacksmith, in a joyless pursuit.

Parigraha, or covetousness, which implies hoarding more and more, is like that "entanglement with 99." The Truth is that happiness is not acquired through the procurement of objects. Multiplying possessions beyond what is necessary does not make you secure. You are ignoring these great truths and adopting the illusion, "If I have more and more I will be happy." Thus, greed is actually a movement in falsehood. So much mental energy is wasted over pursuing the objects of the world. By freeing the mind of this great burden though Yogic disciplines, one can enjoy the inner wealth of genuine peace and contentment.

The Effect of Covetousness on Society

From a social point of view, a person who develops covetousness disturbs the harmony and economic balance of society. Why should one person hoard so much more than he can use, when those things could have been utilized by others? It is unethical that many are deprived of the conveniences of life while others hoard far beyond any reasonable need. Such hoarding negates the fact that the same life flows within all. It is a form of violence. You are hurting others by developing exaggerated desire, and causing imbalance and disharmony in society.

On the other hand, if people were infused with the virtue of noncovetousness, the ideal would be simple living and high thinking. The ideal would be to pursue the greater treasures of life, the spiritual values, while material wealth becomes subservient to spiritual wealth. In a more cultured and elevated society, there would be an entirely different kind of desire: A strong desire for the attainment of spiritual virtues. One would crave for more and more sincerity, mental peace, goodness, gentleness and mental serenity. People would be discontented with their psychological and spiritual limitations and strive to become better and better every day!

If this ideal were practiced, there would be peace within every individual who promoted it, and they would radiate happiness and peace in the environment. This would lead to a higher level of culture for the individual and for society.

Chapter Two
The Two Greatest Commandments of Christ

In the New Testament a man approached Jesus, asking, *"Master, which is the greatest commandment in the law?"* Jesus gave the essence of His teachings in the following statements,

> **Thou shalt love the Lord thy God with all thy heart, and with all thy soul, and with all thy mind. This is the first and greatest commandment. And the second is like unto it: Thou shalt love thy neighbor as thyself. On these two commandments hang all the laws and the prophets.**
> (KJB Matthew 22:36—40)

When understood in the light of Yoga, these commandments are seen as shining declarations of the need to practice Integral Yoga in daily life.

Thou shalt love the Lord thy God with all thy heart, and with all thy soul, and with all thy mind.

The Yogic system of mysticism presents four paths leading to the realization of the Self: Jnana Yoga—the Yoga of Wisdom, Bhakti Yoga—the Yoga of Devotion, Dhyana Yoga—the Yoga of Meditation, and Karma Yoga—the Yoga of Action. These four paths correspond to the four aspects of the human personality: Reason, emotion, will and action. In the ideal system of spiritual movement, these four are properly blended and integrated.

An aspirant practices Karma Yoga for the purification of the mind (freeing the mind of hatred, greed, pride and other gross impurities). One practices Bhakti Yoga to perfect one's practice of Karma Yoga on the one hand, and to advance in one's inward devotional movement on the other. Increasing devotion to God provides insight into meditation and *samadhi* (superconsciousness) and, thus, one becomes a practitioner of Raja Yoga. Finally, one's mystical movement attains its fulfillment in ascending the rungs of wisdom or Jnana Yoga and realizing one's unity with the Divine Self.

Bhakti Yoga (the Yoga of Devotion) gives insight into the art of loving God *"with all thy heart."* Jnana Yoga (the Yoga of Wisdom) teaches the technique of loving God *"with all thy soul"* by discovering the true nature of the soul as the Absolute Self. Dhyana Yoga (the Yoga of Meditation) gives an insight into loving God *"with all thy mind"* by the practice of meditation and *samadhi* (superconsciousness).

As you practice devotion, meditation and wisdom in your daily life, the path of Karma Yoga (the Yoga of action) spontaneously unfolds as you fulfill your responsibilities as an individual in society. As you advance, this expresses itself through acts of selfless service of humanity. You discover a level of Universal Love that enables your heart to realize your neighbor and even the entire world as your very self. Selfless service purifies the heart and brings about expansion within your consciousness, helping you advance on the paths of devotion, wisdom and meditation. In turn, as you advance along these paths, you are able to practice Karma Yoga with ever increasing effectiveness.

The teachings of Lord Jesus have thus indicated a glorious blend of devotion, meditation, wisdom and action. These are the same teachings that are taught by every religion and spiritual movement of the world from ancient times. Although these teachings are delivered through different languages and rituals, the message is the same: To attain Liberation—the Kingdom of Heaven—you must love God with all your heart, your entire mind must be captured by

God's beauty, glory, power and majesty, and you must feel that you are serving God in all that you think and do.

Religion is not a matter of a sentimental belief, a verbal confession, or an intellectual affirmation. True religion requires that your total being be completely immersed in the love of God. When God is loved in this way, there is no one else to love. God alone has become your reality.

As a spiritual aspirant, you may at times experience intense surges of higher sentiments, and become overwhelmed by a wonderful feeling that God alone is and that you love Him perfectly. You may even shed tears as these feelings swell within your heart. Although these sentiments are indeed very good, the moment they evaporate you may find that your mind is unable to even think of God or love Him at all. When a feeling that you thought was a deep and abiding devotion becomes a wave of sentiment that passes on, this indicates that your personality has not reached a state of full integration.

Similarly, at times your intellect may achieve a state of clarity, and you may profoundly feel that you understand that all is God—that *Brahman* alone is. However, soon the clouds of confused sentiments block your vision and you find that your clarity of reason has been lost.

At times you may find that your reason and feeling are both presenting a clear understanding of God and true spirituality before you, but you are unable to express it in your day-to-day activities. You find that your ego hinders you from adapting and adjusting to the challenges of the world. When you sit quietly for meditation and prayer, you are aware of God's Presence. But a few minutes later, when someone insults you, angry words come bubbling forth from your tongue like frogs croaking in a lake! Your not-yet-integrated personality prevents you from realizing that you are dealing with the same God in the person who insulted you as in the person who places a garland on your neck. Ego causes you to forget that you are always in the presence of the Divine Self, no matter how distorted a face He presents to you.

Therefore, in order to love God wholeheartedly— not halfheartedly, intellectual conviction is not enough; sentimental feeling is not enough. In spiritual movement there must be a complete integration of your personality in which head, heart, and hand are in total harmony and your whole life becomes ablaze with spiritual aspiration.

With All Thy Heart

Loving the Lord *"with all thy heart"* is the message of devotion or Bhakti Yoga. All your feelings and sentiments flow towards God, as you perceive Him to be the reality in all. It is by loving God and being loved by God that the sentiment of love finds its highest fulfillment.

Devotion or love of God predominates in the teachings of Lord Jesus as well as in many Yogic teachings. In the Vedic scriptures the various Yogas are described, but Bhakti, the practice of devotion, is always given a prominent role because the qualifications are simple: Anyone can kindle love in their heart.

Love is innately present within every individual. Everyone is aware of it, no matter how limited it may be. Therefore, that love can be directed towards God. In the Gita, many different paths are described, but devotion is highlighted.

Love of God should not be shallow. That love should flow like a pure and powerful stream, deep within your heart. Reading the Bible and reciting its prayers and commandments is good, but that is not enough. You have to love the Lord with all your heart, from the very core of your feelings, by integrating all your sentiments and transforming them into Divine Love.

Everyone seeks to love and to be loved, but the perfect object of love and the perfect source of love can never be found in this world. It is by loving God and recognizing the mystical fact that you are ever loved by God that the sentiment of love finds its only real fulfillment.

God is the Reality in all human beings, but due to *Maya* (Cosmic Illusion), one becomes attached to names and forms and to transient personalities. As a result, the Divine Self, Who is the very embodiment of Love, is ignored. Therefore, you gradually learn the art of withdrawing your heart's loving sentiments from the relationships and objects of the world and redirecting them towards the Self.

This movement does not imply that you develop a cold indifference towards your relatives and friends. Rather, it implies that you develop a stronger intensity of love—love that is more elevating and inspiring toward those who love you and toward those who are loved by you. When you love the ocean, the waves are automatically included. In the same manner, when you love God, the transient names and forms of the world (all living and nonliving things), as well as the entire universe, are all automatically included. This is expressed in Christ's statement,

> **But seek ye first the kingdom of God, and his righteousness; and all these things shall be added unto you.**
> (KJV Matthew: 6-33)

By the practice of *japa* (repetition of mantra or Divine name), prayer, devout meditation, and association with Saints and Sages, you learn the art of developing love for the Supreme Self (God). This is the essential teaching of all the religions and spiritual movements of the world.

With All Thy Soul

To love God *"with all thy soul"* relates to the path of Jnana Yoga, the Yoga of Wisdom—the path of reflection and enquiry. As an aspirant, you listen to the teachings of the scriptures and begin to understand the nature of your individual soul. Through reflection and meditation, you fathom the depths of your personality to discover the soul that is the source of your ego. As your reflection and meditation deepen, you gain insight into the fact that your innermost soul is different from the body, mind, senses, and ego. That soul is the soul of the entire universe. It is identical with the Supreme Self. You attain the intuitional vision that leads to the direct realization, "I am That—the Absolute Self." This is expressed in the statements of Christ, *"Is it not written in your law, I said, Ye are gods?"* (John 10:34) and *"Behold, the kingdom of God is within you."* (KJV Luke: 17-21) These statements point to the essential teachings of Vedanta philosophy: The essential identity of every individual is the same Absolute Self. Realizing that identity by discovering your innate Self is the goal of the path of Jnana Yoga, the Yoga of Wisdom.

With All Thy Mind

Loving God *"with all thy mind"* refers to Dhyana Yoga—the Yoga of Meditation. Through the practice of concentration, meditation and *samadhi* (superconsciousness), you learn to gather the multiple rays of the mind and allow them to flow uninterruptedly towards the Divine Self.

The mind in most people is scattered over the transient objects of the world. Numerous thoughts rise and fall in the lake of the mind. People are perpetually involved in the thoughts of yesterday, today, and tomorrow. They are unaware of the immense joy that arises when the mind has been freed from its restless thoughts, and like a tranquil lake, it reflects the majesty of the Divine Self.

When you learn the art of withdrawing the mind from the world-process and directing it towards God, you experience immense joy. The thoughts arising in such a mind are most powerful and promote peace, prosperity and harmony in the world, inspiring humanity for many centuries to come.

Thou shalt love thy neighbor as thyself.

When Lord Jesus was asked, "Who is my neighbor?" he responded by giving the following parable:

As a man was going down from Jerusalem to Jericho, robbers attacked him and grabbed everything he had. They beat him up and ran off, leaving him half dead. A priest happened to be going down the same road.

But when he saw the man, he walked by on the other side. Later a temple helper came to the same place. But when he saw the man who had been beaten up, he also went by on the other side.

A man from Samaria then came traveling along that road. When he saw the man, he felt sorry for him and went over to him. He treated his wounds with olive oil and wine and bandaged them. Then he put him on his own donkey and took him to an inn, where he took care of him. The next morning he gave the innkeeper two silver coins and said, "Please take care of the man. If you spend more than this on him, I will pay you when I return."

Then Jesus asked, "Which one of these three people was a real neighbor to the man who was beaten up by robbers?" The teacher answered, "The one who showed pity." Jesus said, "Go and do the same!" (CEV Luke 10:30-37)

In this parable, the Good Samaritan, by showing compassion towards a robbed and beaten stranger, was considered by Christ a better man than those who passed by and ignored the unfortunate individual. To the Samaritan the injured traveler was not a stranger, but one to be served and cared for as a dear neighbor.

Therefore, when Lord Jesus uses the term "neighbor," He is not referring to someone who lives or works in physical proximity to you. You can be physically distant from people, although they are very close. You can be in physical proximity to others, and yet they are distant. So it is not physical closeness that makes someone a neighbor.

Rather, *"Love thy neighbor as thyself"* speaks of the ideal of universal Selfhood. It is the recognition that the same Divine Self that underlies your personality underlies all personalities. If the human personality is a wave, the innermost core of that personality is the Ocean—and that Ocean of God is the Reality within every individual. God alone exists as the Indweller of all.

There is an interesting story about Ramana Maharshi, a great Sage in India, who demonstrated this sublime teaching. One day, thieves invaded his ashram, stole an assortment of valuables and beat him. Seeing this, an outraged disciple said, "I am going to find those thieves and break their necks!" However, Ramana Maharshi said, "Do not do so! If your teeth were to bite your tongue, would you knock them out? No, you wouldn't, because they are a part of yourself."

Similarly, it is possible for you to develop the awareness that every being is as much a part of yourself as your teeth, fingers, or toes. The moment you view the world as an organic whole, you become One with all. How can there be selfishness, anger, greed, and various other complexities in such a mind? If the mind glimpsed the essential unity that underlies all, if it recognized the Divine basis behind all names and forms, it would be free of every trace of violence and hatred.

If Christ's vision of universal love is promoted, all that is auspicious will flow from that vision. Realizing the Divine harmony and universality of life is an attainment more glorious than climbing Mt. Everest and more exhilarating than stepping onto the moon. It is more powerful than nuclear bombs, and more enduring than time itself.

Universal Love is the foundation and support for all spiritual virtues. That is why Buddha gave great emphasis to the teaching: *"Ahimsa Paramo Dharmah"*—"Nonviolence is the greatest of all virtues." Patanjali Maharshi also gave prominence to nonviolence and considered it as the basis of all other *yamas* (restraints) and *niyamas* (observances) on the path of Raja Yoga. This is also well expressed in the Biblical writing:

> ***Owe no man anything, but to love one another: for he that loveth another hath fulfilled the law...if there be any.***
> (KJ21 Romans 13:8-10)

Thus, one test of your spiritual attainment is your ability to feel profound unity with all. When you authentically follow your spiritual path, there is an abiding sense of universality. Just as you are interested in removing your own discomforts, you begin to recognize others' pain and your heart flows with compassion towards alleviating that pain as well.

As this vision unfolds, you are filled with profound universal love and compassion. You discover all humanity to be your neighbor. Indeed, this insight is not limited to humanity. It includes all forms of life; it includes the entirety of creation. The term "neighbor" is a symbol for all that is. All becomes yourself, and you love all as the Self.

As we have seen, Lord Jesus sums up all the commandments in these brief statements:

Thou shalt love the Lord thy God
with all thy heart (devotion)
and with all thy soul (wisdom),
and with all thy mind (meditation)
as well as
Thou shalt love thy neighbor as thyself.
(selfless service of God in all)

In a similar fashion, in the Bhagavad Gita (XVIII—65), Lord Krishna says:

Let your mind be absorbed in me (meditation),
be devoted to me (devotion),

> *sacrifice for me* (action),
> *bow down to me* (surrender).
> *You will come to me* (wisdom);
> *Truly do I promise unto you*
> *for you are dear to me.*

Thus, a true follower of the teachings of both Christ and Krishna, as well as a true follower of all religions in their essential purity, will bring about a blend of the four aspects of Integral Yoga in their daily life. Lord Jesus was a fully blossomed Yogi, and all four Yogas find their culmination in His glorious personality.

Chapter Three

The Perfection of Divine Love

In the course of His most precious teaching of the Sermon on the Mount, Lord Jesus said,

> ***Be ye therefore perfect, even as your Father who is in Heaven is perfect.***
> (KJV Matthew 5: 48)

But what does it mean to be as perfect as God? Consider how God showered His attention and artistic talent even upon the smallest of His creations. Look at a butterfly that lives for only two or three days—how intricately beautiful are its wings! At the same time, He bestows the same attention on the planets and stars. His perfection is beyond imagination. Observe how abundantly the sun bestows its rays on all—those who praise it and those who curse it. It never selectively withdraws its rays. See how the sandalwood tree emits the most aromatic fragrances when struck with an axe. These convey the secret messages regarding the perfection of Divine Love.

Divine Love expresses and even transcends patience, endurance and magnanimity. It inspires you to bless those who curse you and pray for those who hurt you. Human love, on the other hand, is painfully limited. It is a love that measures. Divine Love allows no space for thoughts such as, "I have helped that person for such a long time and given him so many gifts; how dare that person not be nice to me in return." For this reason, Lord Jesus says, *"Be ye therefore perfect, even as your Father which is in Heaven is perfect"*—not perfect as a human being.

There is always limitation in human virtue, but an aspirant transcends it. To maintain constant effort in surmounting one's limitations is the beckoning light of Christ's teaching. Without magnanimity of heart, one cannot surpass the world and attain the Kingdom of Heaven, the highest victory in life.

Divine perfection should be kept before your mind as your ideal. Most people do not have a mystical grasp of the concept of perfection. There are many "perfectionists" in the world who throw aside or destroy their work if it does not meet their expectations. The perfectionist writes a letter to his friend, only to tear it up because it is not good enough. Of course one should always try to do one's best, but too much involvement in being perfect in selected fields of life is not the mystic perfection of which Lord Jesus was speaking.

Real perfection has to do with exploring your inner life and removing fear, insecurity, and the complexes that cause you to develop ill will towards others. These are the clouds that obscure the shining moon of Divine Love. When you reflect upon what lies within your heart and begin to remove these obstacles, then you are moving towards genuine perfection.

Love One Another as I Have Loved You

A new commandment I give unto you: That you love one another, as I have loved you. By this shall all men know that you are my disciples... (KJV John 13: 34-35)

The movement in Divine Love must be twofold: internal and external. Internal disciplines, such as meditation and prayer according to your own religion or faith, should be practiced regularly in order to awaken and nourish love for God. But equally important is the attention you give to how you interact with other people around you. If you truly love God, then your love for Him expresses itself through loving kindness towards His whole creation.

In other words, love of God does not involve merely closing your door and practicing your own personal spiritual disciplines. It implies an ability to express a Divine feeling within your heart towards others, an ability to assert the power of love over hatred, an ability to wait and watch, and an ability to do little things in day-to-day life that carry a fragrance from Heaven.

And what are those little things? In the words of Saint Francis of Assisi:

> *Lord make me an instrument of Your peace.*
> *Where there is hatred, let me sow love.*
> *Where there is injury, pardon.*
> *Where there is doubt, faith.*
> *Where there is despair, hope.*
> *Where there is darkness, light.*
> *Where there is sadness, joy...*

It is the little things that one does day by day that are like jasmine flowers. Though they are small and delicate, they carry a rich fragrance that sweetens your life. If your actions promote harmony, peace, and joy, then you are praising God and serving Him through your goodness to others. Even the smallest type of action, such as making another person more comfortable, or less afraid, or more cheerful becomes a form of prayer—prayer that is active and dynamic, prayer that has true depth and meaning.

When you express your love for God in this way you become a great practitioner of nonviolence. In spite of negative situations or external provocations, you continue to assert your goodness. As a result, you see negative people transformed into positive, inimical into friendly, demoniac into Divine. To the extent you are able to contribute to that movement you experience a majestic revelation in your life.

A Saint perceives all living beings as his neighbors and spontaneously performs actions for universal welfare. For you to grow in saintliness, the great ideal of loving your neighbor as your very self must always be kept before your mind.

Imagine the difficulties others must handle. Help them with sympathy and compassion. It is a great spiritual art to place yourself in the shoes of another person. As the heart becomes increasingly purified, your feelings are no longer cramped by anger, hatred and selfishness. Therefore, you understand people deeply and help them effectively.

When you cannot tolerate discomfort and pain within yourself, you find a remedy. Similarly, feel the pain in others and find a solution according to your capacity. Qualities such as charity and compassion should not be limited to your family. Those qualities should be extended towards all. If your magnanimous feelings remain limited to your friends and relatives, then those feelings become polluted. Water that does not flow becomes stagnant.

Nothing purifies the personality as effectively as the performance of actions for the benefit of others. The Mahabharata states, "Virtuous deeds directed towards others are the essence of righteousness, while mistreatment of others is the essence of unrighteousness."

Never procrastinate on following through on kind thoughts or ideas. Respond quickly from the goodness of your heart. On the other hand, postpone your negative reaction to circumstances. If you have suddenly developed some type of dissension with another person, and your mind plans to sharply criticize, hesitate. Say, "Tomorrow I may write a harsh letter to that person, but for now I'll just wait." In this type of practice, mind gains amazing powers of forbearance and patience.

In normal human relationships, if someone does something good to you, you feel very joyous and in turn respond with kindness. That is only normal. However, the goal of spiritual movement is not mere normalcy, but a supernormal pursuit of Divine perfection. Thus, if someone has attempted to harm you or cause pain, reciprocate with sincere goodwill, and if the opportunity arises, do something that will inspire the person. That is the ideal aspiration. The moment you begin to follow that ideal, you are treading the path to becoming as perfect as God.

Sow Flowers instead of Thorns

Saint Kabira sang:

Jo tokon kaantaa buvai taahi boi too phool,
Tokon phool ke phool hai, vaako hai tirshool.

> "If you sow flowers for those
> who have sown thorns for you,
> there will be nothing but flowers for you.
> But for them there will be a piercing spear."

What does this imply? Suppose someone pulled out all your wonderful plants during the night, and in their place planted thorny bushes around your yard. What should you do? The normal reaction would be to take all those thorny bushes back to his garden, and when he is sleeping plant the spikey bushes in place of his lovely ones. This is the philosophy of tit for tat, an eye for an eye, or a tooth for a tooth. If this degraded philosophy was put into practice as often as many would like, surely the world would soon become eyeless and toothless!

But if you aspire for the ideal of Divine perfection, you will smile within yourself at the act of that inimical person, at how much hatred exists within his heart. You will realize that such a person is deprived of his inner peace, and you will be determined to have a positive influence upon the person. So while he is sleeping, you will find the best flowers and plant them in his yard. He sowed thorns in your garden, but you sow beautiful flowers in his. Because, when he sees what you have done, he will sincerely see his error, and feel the "punishment" for his actions more severely than you could have imagined.

If someone has erred and you give him a big slap, he will not understand his mistake. What he feels is the pain from your slap. But if you respond with goodwill, he may see the contrast between his behavior and yours and recognize his error. Though it is not intended as such, this is a far more effective "punishment."

Bless Them that Curse You

Bearing insult and injury requires constant vigilance and is a great aspect of *sadhana* or spiritual discipline. Urging His followers to emulate the perfection of Divine Love, Lord Jesus states in the Sermon on the Mount:

> *I say unto you, love your enemies, bless them that curse you, do good to them that hate you, and pray for them which despitefully use you and persecute you; that you may be the children of your Father who is in heaven; for He maketh His sun to rise on the evil and on the good, and sendeth rain on the just and on the unjust. For if you love them that love you, what reward have you? ... Be you therefore perfect, even as your Father in heaven is perfect.* (KJV Matthew 5:44-48)

This ideal may seem impossible to most people, but when your goal is to attain Enlightenment, the virtue you practice has to be extraordinary. The normal, ordinary virtue is to love someone who has been good to you and to hate the person who has harmed you. To aspire to be a Godlike personality requires that you practice virtue of a different type: to be as perfect as God.

Lord Jesus reminds us how God allows the sun to rise on the good and evil alike. If God were sentimental, imagine how things would be. If He felt that you were not following His commandments, He might withdraw the sun one day and allow it to rise only for those whom He recognized as good. But it is not so; the sun shines upon all. Those who condemn God as well as those who praise Him find the sun flooding into their homes whenever they open their windows. The air tenderly enfolds everyone. Oxygen enters your nostrils whether you hate God or not. Therefore, if such is the nature of God, such should be the nature of His devotee. Strive to be as perfect as He is.

To be perfect implies that even if you are placed in an adverse situation, your mind will enjoy the sweetness of Divine Love. Although you may be treated crudely, inwardly you are unaffected and inspired to bless the person who wrongs you.

In the Vedic scriptures, the metaphor of sandalwood is often used. If you strike a sandalwood tree with an axe, you will find that the sandalwood responds by imparting a bit of its fragrance. Such is the nature of a Saint. That ideal must be kept before your mind so that your personality may bloom into perfection. But when you do not hold that ideal, you live in the world of ignorance, where revenge, ill will, and irrational hatred abound. In that world, life becomes shallow, religion a mockery, and prayers hypocritical.

When you act on the basis of "an eye for an eye and a tooth for a tooth," and long to see your enemy crushed, your mind becomes degraded. Perhaps you quarreled with another person and he spoke harsh and hostile words. Later you hear that he has slipped on a banana peel and broken his leg; so you say, "How wonderful!" That kind of reaction makes you imperfect. If you hold that hostility within yourself, it erodes your vitality and harms you instead of your enemy. Such thoughts lead you to a lesser, degrading state of existence, and eventually to lingering unhappiness.

In movies you see how the "hero" pursues his enemy seeking revenge—and he usually succeeds. If the hero had one tooth broken by an adversary, he doesn't break just one tooth of his enemy, he breaks all of them. But that is not real heroism. If you follow that ideal, you become internally humiliated. It may give you a real sense of justice for the moment, but the truth about your immature attitude eventually reveals itself and sorrow begins to cripple your mind.

If you are a true hero, you build mental and emotional strength by discovering tremendous patience, intense endurance, and unconditional forgiveness under all provocative conditions of life. Your profound spiritual strength allows you to maintain an aura of dignity under all circumstances by never feeling insulted. You realize at a deeper level that your apparent enemies are only Divine Will testing you through different personalities according to your karma. And although it is not always easy to understand, those tests are a blessing from a loving God whose intention is to lead you on to increasing mental purity and eventually Liberation!

As Saint Kabira expressed so eloquently, those who are hostile to you are not to be shunned. Rather, they are to be loved and cherished:

Nindak niyare raakhiye angan kutee chhavaay.
Binu paani sabun binaa nirmal karai subhaay.

"Keep the fault-finder very close to you.
Give him a well-furnished room.
He will help you to purify your nature
even without the use of soap and water. "

Compete with Yourself in Developing Divine Qualities

Ye have heard that it hath been said, An eye for an eye, and a tooth for a tooth: But I say unto you, That ye resist not evil: but

whosoever shall smite thee on thy right
cheek, turn to him the other also. And if any
man will sue thee at the law, and take away
thy coat, let him have thy cloak also.
(KJV Matthew 5:38-40)

Developing positive qualities is essential for attaining Divine perfection. There should be no limit placed on promoting good qualities. Rather, compete with yourself. If you have been humble throughout the last year, try to be humbler still. Persevere until you excel, instead of comparing yourself to others.

In most systems of spiritual practice, moderation is the law; but in the development of virtue, excess is admirable. Ever dare yourself to go a little beyond. That is what Lord Jesus implied in the above statement: When someone slaps you on one cheek, give him the other. To have taken one "slap" without saying anything is good, but to offer your other "cheek" is Divine. These instructions are not meant to be taken literally. Imagine a Christian who has been robbed of one article of clothing running after the thief, exclaiming, "Excuse me, sir, you missed this one!!" While it is necessary to hold people responsible for their negative actions, it is not necessary to harbor hatred or ill will towards them.

Being able to maintain a loftier inner attitude is the spiritual challenge. The implication is to practice your virtue to excess. If you are aiming at an archery target, you always aim a little higher so that the arrow hits the target. Similarly, when you are aiming at developing spiritual qualities always aim higher. Always have a surplus of virtue.

Reconcile Your Differences with Others

To emphasize the glory of maintaining harmony, Lord Jesus said:

So if you are about to place your gift on the altar, and remember that someone is angry with you, leave your gift there in front of the altar. Make peace with that person, then come back and offer your gift to God.
(CEV Matthew 5:23-24)

If, at a time of ritual worship, you remember someone with whom you have argued and had disagreements, "forget" about God and run to that person and reconcile your differences. Only then should you return to worship God. If you pray to God while holding ill will towards the people around you, God will not be pleased. God is the Indweller in all. If you hold ill will towards others, you hold ill will towards God. You must settle matters with your neighbors and relatives before coming to worship God, for if you hold a grudge against them your worship will lose its efficacy.

If, at the back of your mind, bitterness is simmering, your turning to God is superficial.

Only in an atmosphere of harmony can worship be the joyous experience it is meant to be: The joy of coming home for a glimpse of God.

An aspirant understands that spirituality is not a private, egoistic pursuit. You cannot simply shut your door and say, "I have become spiritual and I do not need any of you." The purpose of spirituality is to shed all defects and negative qualities from your personality and develop positive ones. Therefore, harmonize with the people in your life. Adapt and adjust so that your mind is not perpetually cluttered with regrets and fears that stem from how you have interacted with those around you.

"Blessed are the peacemakers for they shall be called the children of God." Peace, not disharmony, must be promoted within and around yourself.

Adapt and Adjust

Living with human beings requires a certain art of adapting and adjusting. It is unnecessary to create conflict over things that have very little meaning or to contradict others over trifles. In one story about King Akbar and his witty minister, Birbal, someone gave a dish of eggplant to the king, who expressed his great enjoyment after eating the preparation. Hearing this, Birbal replied, "That's why God has put a crown on its head." But the next day the king complained that the food had given him indigestion. Birbal replied, "That is the reason God drove a nail through its head." "Why," Akbar asked Birbal, "Did you previously say that God put a crown on the eggplant, and now you are saying He drove a nail through its head?" "It's very simple, Your Majesty," Birbal replied. "I am your servant, not a servant of the eggplant."

Similarly, in living with other people, be a servant of the Divine within them. Promote happiness around you and try not to create dissension over small matters. Thereby, your mind will not waste its energy, but rather remain bright and joyous. This is one example of artistic techniques that promote the positive in your unconscious.

On the path of spirituality, the life of an aspirant presents many opportunities to adapt and adjust. By learning the art of conforming to situations in a harmonious way, you become a personality that can move in the world easily and effectively. You are able to bow down to the Divine in others without ever losing your own Divine integrity.

Four Attitudes for Promoting Harmony

Raja Yoga teaches four special attitudes that promote harmony in your interactions with others around you:

Mudita or cheerfulness is a *satwic* technique to develop when you observe someone who has far excelled you or who is superior in knowledge or achievement. You feel a sense of joy because the other person is reminding you of your own potential to achieve greatness.

Maitri is friendliness towards those who are similar to you in spiritual attainment. Adopt a *satwic* attitude when meeting with them instead of developing the *rajasic/tamasic* qualities of competition, jealousy, and hate. Their happiness is your happiness; their success is your success. When you observe someone resolving a problem, or practicing meditation and devotion, you should appreciate their efforts. If, in the spirit of *satwic* competition, you attempt to exceed their spiritual efforts, you will not diminish the other person in any way by your own efforts.

Karuna, or compassion, is a Divine quality to cultivate when meeting those people who are struggling with obstacles and committing errors you have already overcome. Instead of viewing those people as inferior because they remind you of your own struggles or pain, be compassionate. For when you were once in their place, you needed people's compassion. Now you are in a situation to direct your compassion towards those who are distressed and to alleviate their suffering.

Upeksha is characterized by indifference. If you were to encounter negative types of individuals who are crude or highly uncivilized, such as thieves or murderers, it is important not to encourage them by reacting to their negativity. Rather cultivate *upeksha* by appearing dumb and deaf. Do not oppose them. This discourages these types of personalities from having fun at your expense. Also, if others target you in an irrational way, become indifferent rather than reacting. Staying quiet does not mean that you are a spineless jellyfish; it means you are utilizing the sublime art of suppressing negative impressions and allowing the positive ones to flourish.

The Mystic Intoxication of Divine Love

There was once a devotee of God in the Middle East who prayed every evening on a mat outside his home. One night, as shadows enveloped the earth and darkness gradually descended, a woman stumbled over his prayer mat while he was reciting his prayers. Furious at the disturbance, he shouted, "You there! Look what you've done! You have defiled this prayer mat by stepping on it with your muddy, soiled feet!"

Surprised by this outburst, the woman cried, "Who are you? Can you really be a lover of God? Is God so uninteresting to you? How it is that Divine Love does not enrapture your mind? In this worldly love, my mind is so enchanted with the thought of meeting my lover that I am unable to see anything. That is why I did not see you or your prayer mat. You are supposed to be a devotee of God! Yet you are more captivated by your ragged prayer mat than you are by Him!" The man then realized that although the woman spoke harsh words, there was great Truth behind them.

If you were to truly practice your religion, intense love of God would so enrapture your heart that you would not be thrown off balance by little problems or disturbances that arise in life. The love of God is a majestic achievement, an experience that one cannot easily imagine. Even a glimpse of that experience can make a person "mad"— with a mystic intoxication belonging to Sages and Saints.

Chapter Four
To Forgive Is Divine

There is a well-known saying that "To err is human but to forgive is Divine." It is the goal of spiritual movement that a human being not remain "human," but become Divine—rising above normal human limitations and unfolding the dormant wings of magnanimity within his heart. One great quality that truly transforms a person into a Divine being is forgiveness, known in Sanskrit as *kshama*.

To become forgiving in nature, you do not have to forcefully plant the virtue within your heart. You need only clear away the impediments that prevent your inherent Divinity from unfolding and expressing itself. The soul in its essence is the embodiment of all virtues. Virtue is intrinsic, while vices develop because of obstructions that obscure one's essentially Divine nature.

If electrical power, which normally serves you in so many beneficial ways, transforms into short-circuited energy, it becomes dangerous. In the same manner, if the natural energy of the soul that spontaneously expresses in the form of virtuous qualities becomes short-circuited, it manifests as negativity. For example, think of the various circumstances when you have become angry because you expected a positive situation and instead experienced a bitter one. That anger developed because of your misunderstanding of that experience and how it could benefit your spiritual growth. As a result, your energy became short-circuited.

In the scriptures negative qualities are represented as demons, positive qualities as gods. These two are in a constant battle. The heavenly world is never at rest. In the Mahabharata, when Krishna beheaded the terrible demon, Shishupal, a light emerged from the body of Shishupal and melted in Krishna. The mystical implication of this scriptural event is that when you destroy the negative, you have corrected the short-circuit, and the tangled energy now flows in a constructive manner.

When the scriptures urge us to unfold Divine qualities and control the negative ones, this does not imply that we should become incapable of such feelings. Anger, agitation and expectation are important aspects of the human personality, and without them we would be like a lifeless painted picture.

Instead, agitations of the mind should be under the control of your reason. A mother training a child may show anger, but she never loses sight of the love that she has towards the child. Under the umbrella of love, you allow firmness and harshness to develop with control, so that anger in itself is not an energy that overpowers your intellect. On the other hand, any form of agitation that stifles your reason is negative.

Forgiveness Is the Secret of Greatness

While suffering on the Cross, Lord Jesus calls out:

> *Forgive them, Father, for they*
> *know not what they do.* (KJV Luke 23:34)

In these resounding words, Christ directed His unconditional goodwill even towards those who crucified Him and revealed the amazing magnanimity of His heart. One who is enlightened possesses a gracious forgiving nature that expresses at all times, no matter what the circumstances may be.

Highlighting the same spirit, the Puranas of India recount an interesting story about Sage Brighu. In early times, there was a discussion among the gods about who should be worshipped as the greatest among the three deities: Brahma the Creator, Vishnu the Sustainer, or Shiva the Destroyer. Eager to settle the question, great Sage Brighu said he would take

up the experiment of testing the three deities to prove who was the greatest among them.

Reflecting within himself, he thought, "I will consider him the greatest who is endowed with unparalleled forbearance and has the greatest control over his temper." With this idea in mind, Brighu first proceeded to *Brahma Loka*, the heavenly region where Lord Brahma dwelled.

Once there, Sage Brighu walked past Lord Brahma without touching his feet and offering the traditional adorations. Brahma could not tolerate the misconduct of the Sage. His eyes grew red with anger and he was about to pronounce a curse on Brighu. Then Goddess Saraswati, Brahma's Divine consort, restrained him, saying, "O Lord, do not be angry with Brighu. He has always been courteous before. There must be some explanation for his behavior." Brahma was thus dissuaded and Brighu quickly slipped away.

Scarcely believing that he had escaped, Sage Brighu hastened his steps to Lord Shiva's dwelling. Approaching the great deity, Brighu again did not offer proper adorations. Rather, he began to insult Shiva, saying, "O Shiva, you wear snakes around your neck and keep your body smeared with ashes. Surely you must be mad!"

At this, Lord Shiva grew angry and reached for his trident, ready to hurl it at Brighu. But Goddess

Parvati, Shiva's Divine consort, pleaded for mercy for the Sage and Shiva reluctantly agreed—at least for the time being.

Fleeing from Lord Shiva, Brighu proceeded to Lord Vishnu's abode. Lord Vishnu, the indweller of every heart, knew what the Sage's intentions were. So even before Brighu arrived, he pretended to be in deep sleep. When Brighu saw Lord Vishnu lying there so peacefully, he kicked the chest of the deity, saying, "You who are the sustainer of the world, how dare you sleep and ignore the well-being of the world!"

In response, Lord Vishnu woke up and immediately clasped the feet of the Sage, saying, "O Sage, your tender lotus foot has been injured by my rock-like chest. What a great sin I have committed. Please forgive me!"

Sage Brighu was amazed at the humility of Lord Vishnu. He said, "Oh Lord, it is I who must be forgiven by you who are supremely compassionate. How can I ever be free of my sinful act of having kicked your sacred chest with my foot? The world will always speak ill of me for having done so."

Lord Vishnu replied, "Oh Sage, on the contrary, the world will sing your praises. You have pleased me by placing your foot on my chest. Just as a mother is pleased even when her infant kicks her, I am ever pleased with my devotees even when they are

---

angry with me. As a token of my satisfaction, I have installed your footprint on my chest. Not only this, every great incarnation of mine throughout the ages will bear your footprint on his chest." Sage Brighu became immersed in Bliss. He had discovered the amazing power of Divine forgiveness.

From a mystic point of view, this story is not meant to ascertain the relative greatness of the deities because, in fact, these deities are really one appearing as three. What it intends to show is the secret of real greatness. The greatness of a person does not lie in his power and prosperity, but in the magnanimity of his heart—his readiness to love instead of to hate, to forgive instead of to bear a grudge, to be humble rather than to be proud and conceited.

The presence of a footprint on the chest of Lord Vishnu's incarnations serves as a mythological reminder of the power of forgiveness. It symbolizes the mystic fact that any aspirant who has truly enshrined Divine humility in his heart becomes a Divine incarnation, an absolute master of his anger and agitation.

Be Alert Not to Develop Pride in Forgiving

Forgiving someone's faults, or forgiving an injury done to you by someone is wonderful, but you should not record how many times you have done so. Do not maintain a mental or written diary that you display before the person enumerating all the good things you have done for them and the number of times you have forgiven them.

Sincere and spontaneous practice of virtue does not amplify egoism or pride. When you strive to display your virtue, it ceases to be virtue. Like a flower bud unfolding secretly in the moonlight, virtue reveals itself with shy spontaneity, sharing its graceful fragrance freely with all.

Wield the Weapon of Forgiveness

What should you do when someone continues to hurt you? The response should not be "An eye for an eye." Ideally, one should learn to conquer evil or misunderstanding with the weapon of forgiveness. The "weapon" one chooses to use in dealing with life's problems is always dependent upon their level of evolution. Grosser weapons are guns, pistols, knives and swords. Subtler and more proficient "weapons" are forgiveness, nonviolence, and love of God.

In normal warfare, if a particular weapon does not become effective, you must invent something more destructive. In the case of spiritual warfare, if the weapon is not effective, you employ something even more Divine. If seven days of forgiveness is not helping you to transform the evil, practice a month of forgiveness. If ten times more forgiveness does not help you to remedy a situation, then practice a hundred times more forgiveness.

Further, if you have done your best and still forgiveness has not brought about a harmonious result, never despair. Your ideal is to attain a mind that remains calm and relaxed and doesn't waste its energy on entertaining hatred. Anger, hated, and jealousy all waste your mental energy and take you away from God within yourself. On the other hand, if you are able to withdraw these negative emotions, you are rewarded with the joy of transformation and a closer relationship to God within.

You gain a power that is so invincible that no power on earth can compare to it. It is the luminous power of love, the power of forgiveness, the power of compassion. As time has passed and history has written thousands of pages of war and murder, the power of love expressing through Jesus, through Buddha, through all the Divine Sages and incarnations shines forth. That power remains the most exquisite source of inspiration for humanity. In that power of love and forgiveness is the resolution to all problems, because it leads to the discovery that "I am the Self in all." In essence, people with different personalities are not really different. They are simply waves within the same glorious ocean of the Self.

Chapter Five

The Meaning of Divine Charity

Charity is a Divine virtue praised in every religious and mystical system of the world. It transforms a human being, purifying the heart, elevating one's thoughts and sentiments, and leading to the Realization of the Self. Therefore, it is most important to gain a deeper insight into the act of charity.

In the New Testament of the Bible, St. Paul speaks of the profundity of charity:

What if I could speak all languages of humans and of angels? If I did not love others, I would be nothing more than a noisy gong or a clanging cymbal. What if I could prophesy and understand all secrets and all knowledge? And what if I had faith that moved mountains? I would be nothing, unless I loved others. What if I gave away all that I owned and let myself be burned

alive? I would gain nothing, unless I loved others. Love is kind and patient, never jealous, boastful, proud, or rude. Love isn't selfish or quick tempered. It doesn't keep a record of wrongs that others do.
(CEV1 Corinthians 13:1-4)

As Saint Paul asserts, you may be magnanimous in words (the "languages of angels"), but if you don't have charity, then all that you express intellectually to the world is of very little value for you or others. You may have developed wonderful intellectual qualities and acquired fabulous possessions, but if you are destitute of charity within your heart, you have gained nothing. Although you may have given all you have, even sacrificing your body, you may still lack real charity. Therefore, you have given nothing and received nothing. What then, is that true charity that the Bible exalts?

Charity is an inner attitude of Cosmic or unconditional love—an attitude that never causes a feeling of inferiority or diminished worth within one who receives charity. Charity allows the recipient to feel joyous while maintaining a sense of dignity and the donor to feel a sense of humility and gratitude.

When you possess an attitude of true charity, you do not judge people, and you are ever ready to forgive. You spontaneously look at the positive aspect of a person, not the negative.

Suppose an awkward guest has come into your home and breaks one of your costly vases. Having broken it he feels frightened, and you tell him that the item has a sentimental value and no amount of money can compensate or replace it. But after your harsh words, you tell your guest that you forgive him because you are a Christian. Wouldn't it have been more charitable to simply tell the person that breaking the vase was unimportant and the incident should be forgotten so that he does not feel degraded about himself? One who is charitable naturally promotes joyousness rather than humiliation in others.

The sun shining above is the epitome of charity. That sun shines on all, those who praise it and those who don't, those who are good and those who are evil. The shining sun allows all to feel free and to unfold their potential. Charity must shine with that same magnanimous feeling or it is not true charity.

The Many Forms of Charity

For the vast majority of people, charity implies giving something material away—giving food and clothing to the poor, serving the sick and contributing to those works that alleviate the suffering of humanity. However, material forms of charity are transient. A hungry man, having received food today, is hungry again tomorrow. Diseases of the body, painful conditions of life, and unfavorable circumstances return again and again. It is indeed virtuous to help mankind with one's material resources, but there are still higher forms of charity to be cultivated and developed within one's heart.

A higher aspect of charity exists within your mental attitude. To understand this point, we can reflect upon another teaching of Lord Jesus: Even when you are hurt by your enemies, hold goodwill towards them. Bless those who curse you; have goodwill towards those who revile you; forgive those who have offended you. This is charity of a truly qualitative spiritual nature.

When you are able to inspire courage within a person who is fearful, when you are able to bring sunshine into a heart that is filled with gloom and despair, when you are able to light a candle of understanding in a clouded intellect, when you are able to encourage anything that is good and Divine in others, that is charity of an advanced order.

Therefore, even if you lack material resources, you can still continue to perform amazing acts of charity. Material charity has a very limited scope, but goodwill sets forth a tremendous force. The force of Christ's charity continues to inspire people today, encouraging them to be generous, self-effacing, enduring, compassionate, and loving.

Another most sublime form of charity is the gift of knowledge, which enables a person to be independent, to discover his hidden talents so that he can improve his circumstances and resolve his own problems. The highest form of charity, however, is the gift of wisdom that leads to Self-realization, thereby freeing the individual from the cycles of birth and death.

Charity in the Light of
Lord Krishna's Teachings

Lord Krishna speaks of three important duties in human life:

1. *Yajna* or sacrifice: Relating oneself with God,

2. *Dana* or charity: One's duty towards other human beings

3. *Tapas* or austerity: The duty towards one's own body and mind, so that his personality may become an instrument equipped with the ability to perform *yajna* and *dana*.

Since God, society and the human personality are deeply interrelated, these three are also closely interconnected. Therefore, from a broader perspective, charity can be austerity and sacrifice. In simpler terms, develop your body and mind in such a way that you are increasingly more serviceable to society. Then you are able to move towards God who dwells within your heart, by sacrificing selfishness, greed, anger, hatred, egoism and other impurities of the mind.

In the Bhagavad Gita, Lord Krishna describes three types of charity corresponding to the three *gunas*:

> *That charity that is given to one who does not reciprocate, which is given with the feeling that it is one's duty to do so, and which is given in the proper place and time to a deserving recipient is considered* satwic *or pure. That charity that is given reluctantly, with the expectation of receiving something in return or with a view of a personal gain is said to be* rajasic, *or impure. That charity that is given at an improper place and time, to an undeserving person and in a disrespectful manner is called* tamasic *or dark.*
>
> (Srimad Bhagavad Gita 17: 20-22).

Of these three, one should avoid charity that is *rajasic* and *tamasic*, and promote charity that is *satwic*. However, many who interpret the Gita literally and are not guided by a spiritual preceptor are unable to understand the significance of this definition of *satwic* charity. They try to look for the ideal holy place, the perfect astrological condition, and a highly deserving recipient in order to practice *satwic* charity. But since they are guided by a subtle sense of miserliness, they are unable to find the conjunction of these three requirements, and ultimately decide to leave all their possessions to their children.

However, when you begin to perform charity under a higher interpretation of the scriptures, the unconscious becomes purified and you begin to draw ideal circumstances to yourself for greater expressions of charity. Therefore, you do not have to look for such ideal conditions. Rather, by merely practicing charity in your daily life in whatever manner possible, you are promoting the highest charity.

Guidelines for the Practice of Charity in Taittiriya Upanishad

About the nature of charity, Taittiriya Upanishad states,

"Give with faith, not faithlessness; give generously; give with a sense of shyness and modesty; give with caution; give with sympathy and love."

Give with Faith: Whenever you give, have faith in righteousness, faith in God within you, and faith in God within others. Develop an understanding that every act of charity is an effective worship of God in humanity. God assumes the form of the poor, the sick, and the downtrodden, and thus offers His devotees opportunities to practice charity and magnanimity in many ways. Thus, by your acts of charity, you propitiate the Divine Self and become endowed with the best of Divine qualities. However, if you lack faith and spiritual insight into the practice of charity, your charity will become *rajasic*. That is, you will be charitable for selfish reasons, and thus continue to intensify your state of bondage.

Give generously: If you are calculating and miserly, your charity becomes *rajasic*. To be sure, you should practice charity according to your capacity; however, develop a sense of openheartedness and magnanimity. Never think that what you have given is too much. Develop the feeling that what you have given is too little, and thereby strive for greater acts of charity. Never feel that you will be lacking as a result of your giving—because the greatest giver is God.

Give with a sense of shyness: Always give with the feeling that you could have done more. Remember that the person receiving your gift may develop the idea that you are the giver, and may become obliged to you—and that feeling of obligation is not desirable. Develop the attitude that the materials you use in your acts of charity do not belong to you, but to God. Therefore, when people applaud you for your acts of charity, you should develop a sense of shyness, a feeling of modesty.

Echoing this theme, Lord Jesus said of charity:

But when thou giveth alms, let not thy left hand know what thy right hand doeth. That thy alms be in secret and thy Father which seeth in secret himself shall reward thee openly. (KJV Matthew 6: 2-4)

This is a figurative way of saying that when you give in charity, do not keep a record in your mind of everything you have given and to whom. Generally, people are tempted to inflate their ego whenever there is an occasion of charity, feeling they have done so much for another. This is wrong. Then your charity has no charity in it.

Give with caution: Be careful not to hurt others with a deluded form of charity. There was a professor who once gave a blanket to a poor man and the poor man, being so overjoyed, blessed him from the depth of his heart. But shortly thereafter, the professor regretted having given away such a costly blanket. He returned to the poor man, took the blanket back and gave him some pennies in compensation. Imagine the pain he inflicted on the poor man by his deluded charity. Instead of creating a positive karma, he created a negative karma. Therefore, one must have a certain sense of caution about the performance of charity, and be willing to eliminate any errors. One must be always ready to reflect within, "Will this person accept my humble gifts? Will I be so fortunate as to be of service to the Divine Self in him?"

Give with sympathy and love: When your act of charity proceeds from a loving heart, its quality becomes highly enhanced. Love adds fragrance to the flowers of charitable deeds. Even the very fact that you can sympathize with other's sufferings makes you a charitable person of high caliber.

By following these instructions given in the Bible, the Gita, and the Upanishads, you practice *satwic* charity; by opposing them, you practice *rajasic* charity. And when your charity results in harming or degrading the recipient, it then becomes *tamasic* and should be shunned. A *satwic* act of charity purifies the giver as well as the receiver. *Rajasic* charity creates the illusions of attachment and hatred between the two, while *tamasic* charity degrades and hurls the performer into the depths of delusion.

According to an interesting parable, God once appeared before a Saint saying, "I am pleased with you; I will therefore grant you the power of healing the sick." The Saint, who was afraid of being caught by the temptation of psychic powers, said, "Oh Lord, please refrain from endowing me with this power so that my mind may flow towards You in an undistracted manner. However, if you must, let my shadow have the power of healing others, and let me be absolutely unaware of that power." The boon was granted, and many sought refuge in his shadow and became healed. But the Sage continued to keep his mind immersed in the loving remembrance of God, unaware that his shadow was performing immense acts of virtue day by day.

Those who are enlightened or Self-realized are truly the greatest performers of charity. This is why the giant shadows of Jesus, Buddha and other enlightened personalities continue to influence millions over the ages. Therefore, whoever takes refuge in their shadows, whoever turns to their teachings, receives inspiration and insight to pursue the spiritual path that brings about the cessation of all sorrows.

It is important for aspirants to remember that merely becoming interested in spirituality and wishing to attain Self-realization does not encompass what is most important. Unfortunately, some may adopt an attitude of, "Why care about the world? Let others go to hell!" But that is a great mistake. The world is your opportunity. People that you encounter are God assuming different names and forms, and it is through their help that you will develop all the positive qualities needed to adorn an evolving personality.

Every soul will one day enter the Kingdom of Heaven. Therefore, develop a charitable feeling for everyone. Furthermore, as you begin to develop such a charitable attitude, your perspective towards your own self becomes magnanimous. You begin to experience true inner tranquility. Charity opens the secret window within your heart, allowing you to soar on the wings of *viveka* (discrimination) and *vairagya* (dispassion) into the transcendental realm where you commune with God.

Chapter Six
The Beatitudes of Lord Jesus

And seeing the multitude he went up unto a mountain. And when he was set, disciples came unto him. And he opened his mouth and taught them, saying:

1. Blessed are the poor in spirit, for theirs is the Kingdom of Heaven.

2. Blessed are they that mourn, for they shall be comforted.

3. Blessed are the meek, for they shall inherit the earth.

4. Blessed are they that do hunger and thirst after righteousness, for they shall be filled.

5. Blessed are the merciful, for they shall obtain mercy.

6. Blessed are the pure in heart, for they shall see God.

7. *Blessed are the peacemakers, for they shall be called the Children of God*

8. *Blessed are they that are persecuted for righteousness' sake, for theirs is the Kingdom of Heaven. For, blessed are you, when men shall revile you, and persecute you, and shall say all manner of evil against you falsely, for my sake. Rejoice, and be exceeding glad, for great is your reward in Heaven, for so persecuted they the prophets which were before you.* (KJV Matthew 5:3-12)

These words, which are generally referred to as the Beatitudes, introduce the Sermon on the Mount, in which Christ presents a summary of His most sublime teachings in a very concise and condensed manner. These teachings of Christ are universal, and of great importance for students of any religion. When you delve deep into the Sermon on the Mount, you will discover the same wisdom that is presented in the Upanishads, Yoga Vasistha, the Vedas, the Gita or in any other scripture of the world.

The Vedas state, *"Ekam Sat vipra bahudha vadanti"*—"The Truth is one, but is spoken of in various ways." Although true religion is Cosmic and universal, each religion uses its own language to express the same great Truths. Each religion is like an aromatic garden, lush with its own special flowers of wisdom that are there to be enjoyed by all.

The more open-minded you are, the greater is your possibility of enjoying the beauty and fragrance of flowers blooming in others' gardens as well.

The teachings of Christ are expressions of a life that is enlightened by Cosmic Consciousness. The characteristics of the life of a *Jivan Mukta* (one who is liberated in life) or of a *sthita prajna* (one who is steady in wisdom) are well portrayed in the life and teachings of Christ and illustrated with particular beauty in these Beatitudes. While in a *Jivan Mukta* the spiritual qualities of the head and heart are as spontaneous and effortless as the aroma of a flower, in the case of an aspirant they are to be developed with effort, persistence, patience, and spiritual understanding.

With this in mind, let us venture into the Beatitudes of Lord Jesus to enjoy their unique flowers of wisdom.

I. **Blessed are the poor in spirit, for theirs is the Kingdom of Heaven.**

Being "poor in spirit" has many mystical implications and is totally different from being poverty stricken in the material sense. Many misunderstand the intent of the teaching when they quote these words from the Bible to console themselves about their inability to succeed in business or to become economically secure. In this way they are confusing "poverty" with the profound mystical concept of "poor in spirit."

Many religious systems have adopted the idea that those who are devoted to God should become monks and not own anything at all. This tradition is based on the understanding that the minds of people who are not highly advanced will be lured into having many possessions. As a result, they will be constantly concerned with those possessions and preoccupied with how to protect and multiply them.

In general, the ideal of simple living and high thinking is always to be valued: Not holding onto more than you need or becoming overly attached to what you possess. However, when you consider external poverty as an end in itself, then you simply remain physically deprived and mentally starved.

With deeper understanding you will realize that people who become materially poor are not necessarily in a better position to develop mental or spiritual advancement. If you are impoverished, you must beg from others and are looked down upon by society.

Further, there are misguided spiritual seekers who hide what they possess from others. When they see others' possessions they say, "Look, he says he is an aspirant, and yet he just bought a new wrist watch! Look, he has no dispassion because he dresses in good clothes and rides in a wonderful car." Falling prey to this error, spiritual aspirants often become proud of possessing less than others and, led by ego, they crave recognition about how little they possess. This is a handicap on the spiritual path.

There isn't a person who doesn't own something in this material world. Even if you owned tattered utensils and a broken hut through which the rains came pouring down, you may still cling tightly to whatever little you own with tremendous attachment. This intense feeling of ownership—regardless of how little or much you own—is what becomes the obstacle to spiritual evolution.

Lord Jesus pointed out that while many religious men emphasize an external form of virtue, He gave a different emphasis. He encouraged the cultivation of the inner roots of virtue, not its external show. Thus, in this Beatitude, it is not external poverty or riches that Jesus was concerned with; it is one's mental state.

When Christ said, *"It is easier for a camel to pass through the eye of a needle than the rich to enter into Heaven,"* he was, on the most profound level, referring to those whose minds were "rich" with complexes, whose minds were burdened by illusions and egoistic concepts. Certainly, those who are rich in that sense will find it difficult to attain Enlightenment.

To be truly "poor in spirit" is a state of mental advancement in which one's mind is so inwardly fulfilled with wisdom that it has spontaneously and totally transcended the objects of the world. It is a state of psychic detachment due to a higher level of mental integration. If the mind is profoundly satisfied, fulfilled, strong, and healthy, it is not attached to the objects, nor does it crave for certain external conditions with the feeling that happiness depends upon them.

Consider life a form of pilgrimage. During pilgrimage it is most important never to carry a big burden. If you carry boxes of overcoats, food, and books, as well as your radio and TV, then the pilgrimage will be painful. You will feel like a donkey bearing a huge load on a mountainous slope. Obviously, the less you carry, the better you are.

Similarly, in this world, if your mind carries burdens of attachment, hatred, anger, greed, and passion, you cannot enjoy the glorious experiences and sights that are there as you journey through life. There are wondrous things that one can learn and observe. However, how can a human being enjoy the greater things of life when all their time and energy is involved in carrying a meaningless burden of impure sentiments?

If a person is travelling on a train and refuses to put his baggage down on the floor, choosing instead to carry the heavy load right on his head, it would seem ridiculous to observers. Then he cannot enjoy the train ride. However, such is the situation with those who are not introduced to spiritual life. They carry the burden of attachment and judgments towards the world wherever they go, rather than simply relaxing in Divine Hands.

In an interesting parable from Indian literature about the life of Lord Krishna, the *gopis*, or cowherd maidens, found themselves standing before the flooding Yamuna River with containers of yogurt on their heads. When the *gopis* found that the flood was so extreme that they could not cross in their usual way, they prayed to Krishna to assist them. In response, Krishna appeared before them with a very small boat. "I will carry all of you across this river," he said, "but only one at a time."

As soon as the first cowherd maiden entered the boat, it began to sink. Frightened, she cried out to Krishna, "Why is it that you cannot take me across? Why does the boat sink?" And Krishna replied, "Because your vessel of yogurt is too heavy. If you throw that yogurt away, the boat will float correctly." And so, she had no choice but to throw away the vessel of yogurt because her life itself was in danger.

Now Krishna rowed the boat a little more, and again it began to sink. Again the maiden said, "What is wrong now? Why can't you carry me across?"

Krishna replied, "The silver jewelry and bracelets that you wear are too heavy." Thus, having no choice, she threw those ornaments away as well.

Again Krishna rowed, and again the boat began to dip, and once more the *gopi* maiden cried out in fear and amazement that Krishna could not take her across the river. This time Krishna showed her that she had to discard even her finest ornaments of gold that she wore. Having done so, she was finally able to cross the river in Krishna's boat.

The parable implies that as long as you are overly attached to possessions you cannot cross the world-process. Your physical body is like the vessel of yogurt. If you are attached to it and unnecessarily preoccupied with its appearance, you must gradually transcend that preoccupation. Your mental indulgences are like silvery bangles, and the subtler desires that burden your unconscious are like golden ornaments. Unless you detach yourself from all these burdens, you cannot cross the world-process and reach the shore of Liberation.

The phrase "poor in spirit" implies the unfolding of *para vairagya*—the supreme dispassion of Raja Yoga. In that lofty state of attainment, the soul, realizing its essential nature, spontaneously does not cling to any material objective. The desires of the mind are dissolved in the supreme fulfillment of Self-realization. Therefore, the spirit does not possess the burden of the world, it is not attached to the shallow waters of material existence, and it is not robed with the tattered garments of illusion.

Vairagya or dispassion develops gradually in the process of personality integration. In the first stage, having pursued many desires, the mind begins to understand that objects of the world cannot give abiding happiness. This understanding enables the mind to control the senses. In the second stage you begin to perceive the degrees of control that you exert upon the senses. In the third stage you begin to control your mind itself and you realize that the world, no matter what it presents, is not going to trouble you any longer.

"Poor in spirit" implies watching your ego to see how it clings to the objects of the world and constantly depends upon them. Though in the practical world you must continue to acquire and protect your possessions, there shouldn't be a deep-rooted psychic involvement in them. Each time your ego clings to objects and external conditions with anxiety, remind your ego that the world is governed by a law much more profound than what it comprehends. Therefore, ego should relax and not fume over things it really cannot control.

In the highest level of understanding, being "poor in spirit" implies that the spirit has freed itself from all its oppressive associations, all its false facades. In Vedantic terminology, the spirit has been separated from the five sheaths (physical, vital, mental, intellectual and causal) and the three bodies (physical, astral and causal). These do not belong to the spirit; they belong to the not-Self.

You have become truly "poor in spirit" when you have attained the intuitive realization that you are not the body, mind, senses, intellect or ego—you are the Supreme Spirit, the Divine Self, the very center and substratum of all that exists. As such, you have nothing to own. Indeed, nothing other than your Self exists. The spirit alone is. God alone is. The Divine Self alone is. This is the meaning of the Vedantic assertion, "Nothing exists. Nothing belongs to me." All that you possessed has vanished. You have realized that they were all illusions. There is utter annihilation of the world-process.

As it is said in Ishavasya Upanishad:

Ishavasyamidam sarvam yatkinchit jagatyam jagat;
Tena tyaktena bhunjithah ma gridhah
kasyaswiddhanam.

"In this great world, whatsoever exists is
permeated by God.
Being united with God, being rooted in God,
renounce and enjoy..."

Just as the ocean permeates all its waves, or gold permeates all golden ornaments, God permeates all the names and forms of this world. God is the only Reality. And that Divine Self should become your goal.

Becoming attached to God is the source of endless joy. As this Upanishad teaches, an aspirant should develop the feeling that God is the reality behind all. Your *bhavana* or devotional feeling should overwhelm the world, stripping it of its reality. The world stands before you with its multiplicity and its turmoils. The ideal is to look at the world entirely as an expression of the Divine Self.

Even before your intellect is able to fully comprehend the meaning of the all-pervasiveness of God, begin exercising your *bhavana*. Allow your feeling to flow towards God through your perception of everything around you. Guided by your sentiments, imagine that it is God's radiance illumining the sun. It is His expansion permeating the sky. It is His profundity surging in the ocean. It is His melody whispering in the breeze. It is His exquisite beauty expressing in birds of the air and deer in the forest. If you have developed that type of sensitivity, then your *bhavana* has encompassed the world, and that magical feeling has overpowered all the discord, disharmony and chaos. The world has become Divine.

The ultimate in religious movement is the intuitive awareness of the universality of the Spirit and the negation of material phenomena. When you have attained that awareness, you are truly "poor in spirit." Nothing exists and nothing belongs to you. This understanding is not reached in a sentimental way, but due to a spiritual expansion that perceives all material phenomena as nothing more than illusion. Since everything is Divine, since everything is God Himself, there is nothing to own. The moment you have nothing to own, you become supremely "poor," but at the same time you are the owner of the Kingdom of Heaven itself. You become One with God, the Absolute, and enter into the Kingdom of Heaven, attaining Liberation or *Nirvana*. All these are different names for the same sublime state in which unlimited bliss and supreme peace become yours forever.

II. Blessed are they that mourn, for they shall be comforted.

For spiritual seekers of all faiths there is great significance in Christ's use of the term "mourn" in this great Beatitude, the second in the Sermon on the Mount. To "mourn," in this profound sense, does not imply a sentimental form of grieving. It does not mean to be always in a state of sadness and gloom.

When you wake up in the morning and feel the beautiful breeze, and see the sun shining on gardens blooming with flowers, you should not become cynical and negative, reminding yourself, "The breeze will not always be this cooling and refreshing; as time passes by, the flowers will wither away, the sky will become overcast with clouds, friends will become foes, and my very body will decay." If you start grieving over the transience of everything in the world in this sentimental manner and continue doing so day by day, your mind will eventually become so negative that you will shut out all possibility of inner joy and peace.

Certainly this form of sentimental negativity would not be encouraged by Lord Jesus or any other Saint who has known the Bliss of God. What then does "mourning" imply? A mind that "mourns" in the advanced, spiritual sense is one that clearly perceives limitation and illusion in all objects and circumstances in this world of time and space. This is not a sentimental feeling, but a deep-rooted understanding that the world with all its best developments cannot really please the spirit, cannot truly satisfy the thirst of the soul.

It is this point that is elaborated in Christ's teachings when He said, *"Foxes have holes and the birds of the air have nests, but the son of man has not where to lay his head upon."* (KJV Matthew 8:20) Because of the all-pervading restlessness and insecurity in the world, the soul is unable to find true rest or satisfaction in anything of the world.

This great world is imperfect, and whatever one possesses will pass away. Everything in this world is ever changing; nothing is substantial or absolutely real. Therefore, the human quest for happiness through the objects of the world is a futile quest. Genuine and fulfilling happiness can never be found as a result of external developments. "Mourning," then, implies promoting a constant understanding that a life confined to egoistic consciousness is a miserable life, a life that is limited and transient. On the other hand, a life that transcends ego and enters into universality is rich and joyous.

You are like a person who once was the ruler of a great kingdom, but now finds himself confined to the desolation of a prison cell. You are intrinsically one with God, yet due to ignorance you have become identified with a body and ego personality. You must realize that being confined within these limits is not your real nature. Thus, your spirit should "mourn" over its confinement and eagerly aspire to become free of bondage by realizing its Divine identity.

The term "mourn" also refers to developing a contrite heart. In addition to perceiving the inherent limitations of the world, an aspirant develops a keen awareness of his own limitations and imperfections as well as a yearning to be free of them. That is the characteristic of an advancing soul. If you are practicing self-introspection, you realize that there is always so much to accomplish. There is never enough compassion, never enough generosity, humility, purity. The moment you begin to feel that you have acquired all the necessary Divine qualities and no longer have any imperfections, your religious movement becomes dull and your spiritual progress obstructed.

Viraha—The Pain of Separation from God

An aspirant discovers a Divine restlessness to be united with the Supreme. You discover the fact that you have been somehow separated from God, from your sweet home, from the Divine Beloved, from the endless ocean of Bliss—and until you become reunited, you cannot rest in peace.

"Mourning" refers to the mystical concept of *viraha* as presented in Bhakti Yoga. A person who develops a spiritual sensitivity realizes he has an internal restlessness that Sages consider the most wonderful attainment in human life. Every human being weeps for nothing, sighs for nothing. But when you become restless for Divine union, when you begin to shed tears due to the pain of separation from God, when your heart struggles like a fish that has been separated from its life-giving waters, then that is the most glorious development for a human being. It is this form of "mourning" that eventually draws to an aspirant the blessing of supreme comfort.

Understanding the limitation of all things, while possessing an increasing aspiration for Cosmic

Consciousness, is what constitutes a truly religious and lofty personality. When you "mourn" with wisdom, devotion, and profound humility, you will experience Divine comfort. As you yearn for God-realization and direct your self-effort towards that attainment, there is a response. However, the mystic path is such that the response from God does not always seem to come quickly. Sometimes you may have to travel a long distance, on a rough road that does not seem to terminate until all your patience has been exhausted. Then, finally, assistance comes from the Divine Hand and you realize that every step you took along the rough road was a form of a blessing.

If you seek Divine union, but still continue leaning upon the objects of the world, God waits to respond. But when you realize that all supports of the world are illusory and you hold onto God alone as your support, then you are comforted. God begins to reveal His grace and provide you with a comfort that cannot be obtained anywhere in the world.

You begin to experience the nectarine sweetness of Divine Presence and feel the Divine Hand guiding all your movements through life. You discover that you do not have to worry about anything, because everything is handled very intelligently by God. Ultimately, when Enlightenment is attained, you gain absolute freedom from grief, restlessness, pain, and misery and experience a sense of eternal satisfaction.

Therefore, the aim of true religion, as taught by Lord Jesus, is not to consider the whole world as an expansion of pathos. Rather, it is to understand that the world is a festivity of God and that it is your birthright to share in that festivity. The purpose of this limited life in the world of time and space is to guide you to the universal experience of the fullness of the Self and the unending festivity of Divine expansion.

As you begin to tread the spiritual path, you will experience some pain in order to free yourself of old egoistic concepts of comfort and joy. In this sense, you are very much like a captive bird that is one day given the opportunity to fly out of its cage.

A bird that has grown up in a cage finds its life very comfortable. Whenever it is thirsty or hungry, someone gives it water and food by opening a little door in the cage, and the bird flutters with great joy. Then one day a person comes along and opens the door and says to the bird, "Come out. You are free." Asked to abandon its present state of security and comfort, and unaware of the joy of freedom, the bird may become frightened of what may lie ahead and be filled with uncertainty. But when the bird flies from its cage, discovering the majesty of its wings and discovering the ecstasy of flight, its previous concept of comfort and joy is spontaneously abandoned.

Similarly, if you have not had a taste of Divine expansion, you may experience sadness in the initial stages of spiritual movement when you are told to become free of the world of limitation. Gradually, however, as you advance and your mind experiences a higher reality, the message of freedom is welcomed, and you are eagerly led beyond your previous limited egoistic concepts to a realm devoid of pathos. When you understand in the depth of your being that the world cannot give you real happiness, your mind relinquishes the burden that it has been perpetually carrying.

Thinking that at some time happiness will be attained, human beings carry bundles of karmas (impressions in the unconscious that result from previous actions, and which give rise to future actions for the incarnating soul). But happiness is not to be found in the karmic burden. It is not in the objects or circumstances of the world. Even if you were to wait for millions of years for happiness in the world, that will never be. Once your mind has profoundly understood that happiness is yours only in the Self, only in realizing who you really are, you become free of the burden of karmic suffering that weighs heavily on human existence.

Chhandogya Upanishad, one of the great, ancient Indian scriptures, asserts that the world with all of its glories is little, or *alpam*. Further, it declares, "*Yo vai Bhuma tat sukham, nalpe sukhamasti"*—"That which is infinite is Bliss; there is no Bliss in the finite." When the mind is illumined with the light of intuition, the world becomes a trifle before the possibility of the eternal glory of the Self. Therefore, devotees of God humble themselves for developing spiritual aspiration and for attaining mastery over the illusions of the world.

They are indeed blessed who mourn over the encircling ignorance that seems to devour human consciousness; and, in so doing, they are lifted to the ever-increasing expansion of Divine Consciousness. When the love of God illumines the human heart, the love of the world fades, until an aspirant at last rejoices in the effulgent expansion of the Self—the abode of infinite comfort and peace.

III. Blessed are the meek, for they shall inherit the earth.

The meekness referred to by Lord Jesus in this third Beatitude is profoundly different from the "meekness" of common parlance. It is not to be confused with the dullness of mind that leads a person to simply accept without questioning whatever the world presents before him. Nor is it the degrading timidity that leaves many people feeling humiliated again and again in life. Certainly it is not the feigned humility that a crafty person adopts to help him get what he wants out of a situation. Such a person may act like a sheep, but he is actually a wolf in sheep's clothing!

The blessed meekness praised by Lord Jesus is a state of advanced personality integration in which one is so profoundly in tune with Cosmic Will that he has no need to constantly assert his ego. Ever guided by the Divine Hand, he carries out the Will of God with total surrender, with the innocent meekness of a sheep driven by the Great Shepherd—God, the Divine Self.

The highest state of "meekness" is reached when a devotee is able to totally submerge his ego and enter into the Ocean of the Divine Self through the intuitive realization of God. This is achieved through a mind that sees the very ego center as merely a reflection of that Self, and not the absolute reality within.

In the lesser stages of spiritual development, the ego center seems to be all that you have, and you are constantly trying to assert the ego. However, as you reflect deeply and enquire into "Who am I?" you gradually realize the illusoriness of the perception of ego, and the vanity involved in being a slave to egoistic consciousness. You eventually understand that the ego is not the all-important factor that it appeared to be, and the tension caused by egoistic illusions gradually begins to subside.

One who is truly meek has developed utter humility. You become a flawless instrument in Divine Hands, without ever egoistically taking the credit for the miraculous results achieved by the Cosmic Will working through you. "How great is this work that I have done!" is never asserted by one who has attained the blessed state of meekness. In the overflowing sense of fulfillment that accompanies your mental expansion, you know that it is not the ego, but the Divine Will that works through human beings, producing great wonders.

The term meekness, in its more practical implication, implies the practice of Karma Yoga. Karma Yoga is a process of spiritualizing all activity with the understanding that your entire life can become an artistic process leading to Self-realization. Imbued with this understanding, you convert every aspect of your work into an act of meditation and prayer.

If you are a Karma Yogi you do not live in contradiction with the karmas or actions that present themselves in your life. Utilizing your intellect, you perform meaningful self-effort, knowing that your personality in the past has already created a karmic process that cannot be ignored or, in some cases, even altered at the present time. This being so, you handle whatever karmic circumstances assert themselves with a sense of duty and respect for the mysterious workings of the Divine Plan. You understand that every karma embellishes your personality, preparing it for greater tasks that will be revealed as you wait and watch with patience.

A Karma Yogi develops the attitude of renouncing or surrendering the fruit of action. Without looking for an egoistic reward or caring whether someone else is there to appreciate your accomplishments, you perform your duties to the best of your ability with an internal sense of integrity. And although your actions may not yield the expected outcome, you continue to perform your duties with patience.

The soul of a Karma Yogi submits itself to God alone. It is not tied to the objects and the circumstances of the world through the strings of desires. Such renunciation of egoistic desires eventually gives you an overwhelming sense of freedom and inner strength, and leads to the blossoming of true meekness within your heart.

The great Indian Saint, Chaitanya, sang:

Trinadapi sunichena, tarorapi sahishnuna,
Amanina manadena kirtaniya sada harih.

"A devotee of God is humbler than a blade of grass,
yet more enduring than a fruit-yielding tree.
He gives honor to others,
expecting no honor for himself,
And he is ever immersed in singing
the praises of God."

These words describe the characteristics of Saints whose spiritual majesty endows them with utter humility and powerful endurance. Just as blades of grass bend willingly and without complaint beneath the feet of those who walk upon them, a person of true meekness submits joyfully to the unfolding of the Divine Will. Just as a mango tree gives its sweet fruit to a child who throws stones at its branches, or a sandalwood tree emits its exquisite fragrance to the very ax with which it was struck, a person of true meekness radiates a spontaneous tolerance and endurance under all circumstances. One who has reached great spiritual heights experiences such an overpowering sense of internal expansion that ego spontaneously loses all its importance.

One who has developed such meekness of spirit enjoys a unique type of relaxation and experiences a joy that so far excels ordinary happiness that it is termed Bliss. The mind is no longer under the grip of selfishness, no longer tarnished by the impressions of frustration and sorrow that accompany egoistic consciousness. The radiantly healthy mind of such a person becomes a basis for intense creative activity that can do immeasurable good for others.

Mind is a form of Divine energy and it is necessary that aspirants use that energy with respect. If you use your mental energy creatively and see that your mind is kept relaxed and cheerful, then Nature courses through your mind creating wonders. Your thoughts become powerful, far beyond your imagination. You begin to enjoy exalted, sublime feelings and sentiments. Through that mind you begin to discover what is really meant by universal love and nonviolence. That mind becomes truly healthy and serves as a source of immense inspiration for yourself and others.

When you develop your mind in this way, it is permeated by the blessed meekness referred to by Lord Jesus, and you "inherit the earth." You become the master of all the circumstances, conditions, and developments within the material world around you. None of these can pressure your mind any longer. Like a lotus, you bloom above all the conditions of the lake of the world and remain untouched by them. Like a swan, you sport in the lake of the world, but at any moment you can flutter your wings, throw off all the water particles, and fly away.

Thus, when true meekness arises, you attain dominion over the material world. The world of matter does not matter anymore. In Vedantic terminology, you triumph over *Maya* or Cosmic Illusion and are no longer tempted by worldly values.

The abundance of the earth is for those who are desireless, not for the man with desires. When a person approaches the objects of the world with desire, he becomes a slave to them. The objects begin to shackle and overpower the person and it becomes impossible for him to possess them in the true sense. But in the state of true meekness, the soul reaches out to God alone. It is not tied to the objects through the strings of desires. Therefore, it recovers its mastery over the earth. It rules matter; it commands circumstances; and it acquires a supreme victory that echoes with an immeasurable sense of inner triumph.

Spiritual movement is a heroic movement, and one who has attained spiritual Realization is like a mighty king. Lord Jesus was so feared by the rulers of His time because He was said to be a "king." In fearing worldly competition, they did not realize that He was not the king of this earth, but the ruler of the promised land of Divine Consciousness. Like the blessed meek of this Beatitude, Jesus had inherited the earth. He had triumphed over the world of time and space and become the emperor of emperors through the miracle of Divine Communion.

IV. Blessed are they that do hunger and thirst after righteousness, for they shall be filled.

The path of righteousness is one that all religions of the world hold in high esteem, as it is the pathway to the Kingdom of Enlightenment. Turning through the pages of history, Christ stands as one of the foremost upholders of righteous conduct. The world continues to stand in awe of the ultimate sacrifice He made for staying true to the Godward path and His commitment to righteousness. Those who hunger and thirst for food and drink do so to sustain their body's needs. Here Christ speaks about that Divine food of spiritual awareness that leads an aspirant to the fulfillment of God-realization.

As aspirants advance on the spiritual path, questions of right and wrong automatically come into play. However, it is very difficult to define righteous behavior in one clear, objective way that all people would agree upon. Different individuals have different standards of righteousness, and labeling something as righteous is often only a comfortable convenience.

For instance, you condemn someone or highlight their faults when you are disappointed or angry with them. On the other hand, when you are pleased, you find a way to minimize their faults and look the other way. Anyone can say another is wrong: "Why should he be so irritable? Why does she act that way towards me? Doesn't he study Yoga or the Bible?" For that matter, anyone could easily assert that Christ shouldn't have done this or shouldn't have done that. Since the rules of righteous conduct are often relative in nature, you must develop increasing wisdom in order to act in the best way possible in any given circumstance.

Further, it is possible to be objectively righteous, yet subjectively confused. For example, speaking the truth is generally considered a great virtue. However, you may say something in the name of truth, hurting many people as you do so, while deep within you enjoy having injured them. Externally you have spoken the truth, but internally you have merely glorified your ego.

According to the most profound teachings of all religions, it is the entry into the universality of existence deep within your consciousness that opens the door to true righteousness. That which is right promotes this universality. Any action, emotion, thought or sentiment that obstructs your movement towards universal life is unrighteous. This must be interpreted by your individual reason and understanding. Tasting the sweet taste of candy is your direct perception. You are your own judge. Similarly, you taste expansion within yourself by your own light, your own mind. Whatever takes you away from that expansion is unrighteous, even if it is clothed in externally righteous garb.

Righteousness Is the Keynote of All Religious Teachings

So in everything, do to others what you would have them do to you, for this sums up the Law and the Prophets.
(NIVUK Matthew 7:12)

But the fruit of the Spirit is love, joy, peace, patience, kindness, goodness, faithfulness, gentleness, self-control; against such there is no law. (RSVCE Galatians 5: 22-23)

Christ, being a Yogi Himself, recognized the importance of spiritual austerity and instructed His disciples to uphold righteous conduct at all costs. In Yogic terminology righteousness is known as *dharma*, and the highest *dharma* emanates from the Supreme Self or God. Unrighteousness or *adharma* stems from the egocentric mind, which continues to create impressions on the basis of selfishness, greed, attachment, fear, anxiety, sorrow, and fleeting pleasures of the world. Raja Yoga further outlines *dharma* in the form of the *yamas* and *niyamas*, such as nonviolence, truthfulness, non-stealing, non-covetousness, contentment, study of scriptures, and surrender to God. The Old Testament of the Bible emphasizes similar virtues in the Ten Commandments.

A life devoted to *dharma* is the very spirit of Yogic culture, and a life devoid of *dharma* becomes meaningless. In Yogic movement, *dharma* becomes the basis of all other pursuits. This is expounded further in the study of basic human ambitions. According to Yoga, every human personality has four major life goals known as the *purusharthas*— the four objectives of self-effort:

1. *Dharma:* Ethical development
2. *Artha:* Material development
3. *Kama:* Vital development, implying human relationships
4. *Moksha:* Liberation

Of the four, *dharma* is considered to be the foundation.

The followers of Lord Buddha outline the Eightfold Path of *Sadachara,* presenting a broad perspective of righteous conduct:

1. *Samyak Drishti*: Right vision
2. *Samyak Samkalpa*: Right thinking and willing
3. *Samyak Vacha*: Right speech
4. *Samyak Karmanta*: Right action
5. *Samyak Ajiva*: Right profession or means for living
6. *Samyak Vyayam*: Right effort
7. *Samyak Smriti*: Right memory (impressions of meditation and spiritual vision)
8. *Samyak Samadhi*: Right form of mental concentration

These eight points, which constitute the Eightfold Path of Buddha, as well as the standards for righteous conduct presented in Raja Yoga, the Bible, and other elevated spiritual teachings, all point to the same Divine goal. Spiritual aspirants of all religions who hunger and thirst after righteousness exist to glimpse the expansion of the Self, and mold their personalities on the basis of such vision. They exist to become a channel of Divine Will and a fountain-source of all that is true, good and beautiful. Thus, truly righteous conduct blooms into the state of *Nirvana* or Self-realization or Liberation—the attainment of the Kingdom of Heaven that exists within every heart.

Every person is essentially the Self. It is due to ignorance that you become oblivious to your own inner glory and become identified with the conditioned spirit reflecting through the medium of the mind. *Jiva*, or the incarnating soul, is a reflection of the Absolute Self. As long as the mind is unable to grasp the majesty of the inner Self, it will continue to weave the fabric of karma for the *jiva*. It is due to limitation that the mind creates the unconscious awareness of individuality and separates itself from the profound oneness of universal life.

Every individual, therefore, is urged by the pressure of truth to discover their essential nature, thereby terminating the cycles of birth and death. Realization of the Self is the highest attainment in the movement of righteousness. *Moksha*, or release from the bondage of the world-process, is the goal of every individual, and is identical to Salvation as mentioned by Christ. The mind holds the key to your own bondage as well as your release. If the cantankerous ego and boisterous senses control your mind, you sink in the marshy lands of illusion. On the other hand, if the mind is guided by luminous reason, you develop excellent Divine qualities and discover the essential Self through intuitive realization.

Saints and Sages—The Model for Righteous Conduct

To understand Christ's teaching of righteousness more completely, it is important to study the minds of Saints and Sages who have attained this exalted state. A mind tuned to the perspective of Self-realization will discover thoughts that are highly ethical and moral. On the basis of those thoughts, one will automatically be inclined to all that is righteous.

Bhagavad Gita tells us:

Yadyad aacharati shreshthas tattadevetaro janah;
Sa yat pranaanam kurute loka stad anuvartate
(3:21).

"Whatever a great man does, others follow. Whatever example he sets, the world emulates."

Righteous conduct is the aroma of Self-realization. As long as the mind of an individual is afflicted by the *kleshas*—ignorance, egoism, attachment, hatred and fear of death—the venom of unrighteousness taints all the movements in life. It is impossible for a person to be absolutely righteous until he removes the ignorance within his heart.

A Sage who is enlightened is not afflicted by the illusion of egoism. His mind is placid and clear like the autumn sky, devoid of the clouds of doubts and desires. That *Jivan Mukta* becomes a flute in the Hands of the Divinity. All that is true, good, and beautiful flows through his dynamic personality. The Vedas, Upanishads, and all other Yogic scriptures have proclaimed the attainment of Self-realization as the goal of human existence; and everything that enables one to move towards the Self is righteous from a broad point of view. Such a movement is a supreme benefit for the individual aspirant, and at the same time, it is the most effective method of raising the standard of culture and civilization in all of human society.

To integrate the teachings of Christ as well as the different aspects of Yoga in daily life, the following points should be reflected upon and practiced for the promotion of righteous conduct in one's personality:

Wherever there is *dharma* or righteousness there is victory. If you adopt the erroneous philosophy that the end justifies the means, you are adopting *adharma*—an unrighteous method—and you cannot succeed in life. Pray and repeat the Divine Name in your daily life. Lift your heart in devotion to Almighty God. Repeat His Name with feeling and devotion. Learn the art of surrendering yourself to God Who abides within your heart. This is the sovereign remedy for all the ills of life.

Seek the Divine Will through your thoughts, words, and actions. Discover the sweetness of Divine surrender. Do not live in tension. Cast off your burdens into the Divine Hands that sustain this entire creation. Spiritualize your actions. Whatever you do, whether in your own home or in your workplace, develop the attitude of worshipping God through your actions. Pray before you commence any work. Conclude with prayer and a short meditation.

Seek *satsanga*, or good association. *Satsanga* is the secret to developing righteousness. Listen to the scriptural teachings from elevated Sages and Saints. Seek the guidance of a spiritual Guru. Promote *satsanga*. Become a moving center of *satsanga* for others. Whenever you work, wherever you go, infuse the spirit of *satsanga* in others by glorifying the Divine Self by maintaining harmony, love, and understanding in your personality.

Develop a healthy mind in a healthy body. The practice of Yoga *asanas* (postures) and *pranayamas* (breathing exercises) are methods for observing the laws of health. Your body is a Divine temple wherein you can discover the Divine Self. Your body is the basis of the fulfillment of the four types of self-effort, and without health nothing can be achieved. Develop insight into a *satwic* diet—a diet that is balanced, nutritious, and has a harmonious influence on the mind. Even a balanced diet must be eaten with a spirit of dedication to God, Who manifests as the gastric fire within one's body. Food is to be eaten for maintaining this Divine temple of the body so that the energy of the spirit can be directed towards the attainment of righteousness and ultimately towards Self-realization. The body should not become a means to unrighteous desires of the mind. A healthy mind in a healthy body constitutes an ideal mystic vessel in which Divine wisdom and devotion can be sustained.

Learn to be adept in *pratyahara*—the withdrawal of the senses. Wherever you may go, there will always be some uncomfortable situation. Withdrawal of the senses allows you to "keep your distance." If you are a practitioner of *pratyahara*, you can enjoy peace and harmony even in a crowded world.

Always strive to create harmony around you. Adapt and adjust to people around you. A little act of self-negation, a little endurance, a little patience, a little inward understanding, a small act of kindness and compassion can remove mountains of misery that arise out of petty quarrels and senseless vanities. People can perform great deeds of generosity with regard to material objects. They may build grand temples and libraries and provide wonderful feasts, but they are unable to offer the most charitable gifts of life—a cheerful face encouraging the goodness in others, a humble spirit that glorifies God in others, and a willing hand that is ready to perform an act of kindness whenever needed. Materially, these things are worth very little, but they are invaluable aids towards the accumulation of the priceless treasure of *dharma*.

Do not delight in revenging upon anyone, even if they are your worst enemy. See the triumph of nonviolence over violence, love over hate. Never compel a person to be good. Learn the art of bringing out the goodness in others through patient persuasion and service.

Practice concentration and meditation in your daily life. Commence your day by meditating on the Divine Self or on any inspirational object of your choice. As time passes, you will discover the deepest secrets of life. Rather than focusing on the defects of your personality, enhance your positive qualities and allow them to prosper. As you evolve spiritually, many negative qualities will be transformed into positive ones. You will begin to discover that you are essentially the Divine Self.

Learn to inquire into "Who am I?" Practice *vichar*—spiritual inquiry pertaining to your essential nature. Study the Bible, Upanishads, Gita, and other scriptures to understand your essential nature—the

Self. Study the teachings of Sages and Saints such as Christ, Buddha, Ramana Maharshi, Ramakrishna Paramahamsa, and others who were constant reminders of Truth.

Become an Integral Yogi—be endowed with a subtle intellect, a melting heart brimming with Cosmic Love, a giving hand, and a self-effacing spirit. See the Self in all names and forms. Gain an insight into the fact that you are not this body but the Imperishable *Atman.*

A lofty plan of conduct has been presented by both the Bible and Vedic literatures. The wisdom that is contained therein is the glorious heritage of all mankind. Allow that wisdom to be explored, practiced, and assimilated for the promotion of happiness, harmony, and peace in this world. As Sage Vasistha says:

He whose conduct is beautiful, whose intellect is endowed with spiritual knowledge, who is no longer attracted to the world and is free of misery—such a person flourishes like an arbor in the spring decked with the fruits and flowers of long life, fame, good qualities, and prosperity.
(Yoga Vasistha: Sthiti Prakarana: 33-60)

The pursuit of righteousness holds the key to the solution of the raging problems of the present-day world. The educational system of today must impress upon the minds of young children the grandeur of a righteous mind as the most important achievement in life. If this were done, they would grow up with the zeal of becoming enlightened Sages. They would not become personalities who act like puppets to the pleasures of the senses and become involved in manifold expressions of unrighteousness. This is the great task before our leaders—the task of presenting spiritual values of life as the foundation of educational systems all over the world.

May all people endeavor to cultivate the glorious qualities of truthfulness, pure love for humanity, humility, compassion towards all living beings, sincerity, absence of anger and hatred, nonviolence, forbearance, purity, non-covetousness, gentleness, discrimination, dispassion, and surrender to God. These are the qualities described by Lord Krishna as *daivi sampat*, or Divine wealth (Bhagavad Gita 16:1-2). Likewise, may all endeavor to eradicate the demoniac qualities of hatred, violence, hypocricy, arrogance, anger, pride, greed, indiscriminate passion, deception, treachery, and all other crude expressions of the lower self, which are called *asuri sampat*, or demoniac wealth (Bhagavad Gita 16: 10-12).

Yato dharma tato jaya—
"Where there is righteousness, there is victory!"

V. Blessed are the merciful, for they shall obtain mercy.

The fifth Beatitude describes another attribute of an enlightened Sage—mercy or compassion. Any person treading the path of spirituality becomes merciful. But the meaning of true mercy or compassion must be properly understood.

The Sanskrit term is *karuna*. In the Vedic scriptures, God is described as *Karuna Sagar*, which means "Ocean of Compassion." To the extent that an aspirant on the spiritual path develops this Divine quality of compassion or mercy, to that extent he is closer to God.

But what does compassion imply? The translation of the Sanskrit term *karuna* is a blend of the English terms compassion, mercy, benevolence, and magnanimity. *Karuna* implies that you are ready to forgive anyone who has harmed you, that you are not eager to judge others harshly, and that you have a tender heart that understands the sufferings of others and an eagerness to alleviate their pain.

What Compassion Is Not

Mercy or compassion is definitely not pity in the ordinary sense. If you analyze your mind, you will realize that when you begin to pity others, there is a bit of a superiority complex. You are developing a sense that, "I am somehow in a better position, and this person is to be pitied." Most people practice this type of mercy. However, the ideal form of compassion is devoid of any egoistic vision.

Certainly it is more positive to express pity (even though backed up by egoistic vision) than to manifest cruelty through one's deeds. However, an aspirant must see the difference between pity and true mercy. A person who expresses pity on the basis of an egoistic sense of superiority intensifies his ignorance, and one who receives such pity humiliates himself in the eyes of his own reason.

Every human being is essentially Divine. Your acts of kindness should not be based upon the illusion that you are all-important to someone, or that they cannot survive without your assistance.

On the other hand, one who gives true compassion and one who receives it are both elevated. It is a mutual reciprocation of the spiritual affirmation that God dwells in all.

Compassion also differs from exaggerated sentimental feelings for others. Such feelings disturb the person who has them as well as the one to whom the sentimental feelings are directed. For example, a mother starts crying when she sees her child injure his finger. Although the wound isn't serious and the child is hardly hurt at all, he sees the tears running down his mother's cheeks and is so moved that he too starts to cry. This is not compassion in the Yogic sense; it is sentimentality. However, even sentimentality is better than cruel-heartedness.

To give another illustration, imagine that you are wading in a river when suddenly you hear a scream and see that the current has caught someone and is pulling him under. Feeling compassionate, you plunge into the water without even knowing how to swim. As a result, both you and the person in distress drown. This is not compassion. It would have been far better had you called someone who knew how to swim. Better yet, you should have learned how to swim yourself so that if such a situation had ever arisen in your life, you would have been able to act more effectively.

Respect other people and treat them with kindness. When they are in distress, sympathize with them and express positive feelings towards them. In so doing, however, one must clearly understand the great difference between a sentimental upsurge to help someone and profound compassion.

Compassion also does not imply perpetual tenderness. Rather, compassion is a profound virtue that permits firmness blended with tenderness. For example, when a surgeon is about to perform an operation, his compassion allows his knife to be sharp, his movements to be precise, and his incision to be as deep as necessary. If he didn't steady his hand or use sharp instruments, he wouldn't be compassionate.

Similarly, when a teacher trains his disciples, his compassion permits him to be firm when firmness is needed, and gentle when gentleness is needed. Think of Lord Krishna in this context. He was tender and firm, always desirous of promoting peace and harmony in the world, yet ready to fight for peace when absolutely necessary.

Compassion Is Based on a Vision of Universality

The entire universe is rooted in the same Absolute Divine Self. Therefore, all beings are linked to one universal life, and other people's sufferings are yours too. Just as you would like to have your sufferings removed, so there should be a spontaneous wish to see others' sufferings remedied as well.

Everyone has that ability to understand the suffering and pain of others with tenderness and sensitivity; however, kindness in most people is in limited degrees and only directed to certain few people. For example, a mother is compassionate towards the suffering of her child, and all the members of a family are compassionate towards the sufferings of each other. However, if somebody next door suffers, it may not matter to anyone. Such "compassion" is limited compassion.

A still more limited form of compassion is the compassion that everyone feels towards oneself. If you do something wrong, you expect others to overlook it. And if they do not do so, you become indignant and say, "How cruel people have become in this world!"

In all these examples, compassion is limited to only a very few people—and if the "compassionate one" is not recognized, surprising cruelty sometimes manifests! But in the case of a Sage, there arises spontaneous compassion for all based on a cosmic vision of the universality of life. This compassion arises on the basis of the knowledge that the entire universe is sustained by one stream of life: "I am all that is."

As an aspirant you must belong to the whole universe. You should not continue to remain confined to a limited vision of family and friends, but discover the ability to commune with all. However, this universal feeling does not imply a cruel indifference towards your relatives and friends. Rather, it enables you to be more profound, sincere and effective towards them as you learn to transcend your egoistic barriers. All are benefited when you realize that you are dealing with yourself when you deal with "others" in the world. Though people seem to be in different physical bodies, in different surroundings, and with different practical realities, they are all essentially the Divine Self that dwells in all.

Karma and Compassion

If people are cruel to you, you must well understand that the cruelty is not entirely from an outer source—it is from the workings of karmic law. Once upon a time, you were cruel to others. Now it returns to you through sources that seem to be completely external.

If you are eager to find fault in others, you must understand that the Divine plan will find fault in you with similar eagerness. That is the way you are creating your karmic process. If you are eager to call others bad names such as "donkey" or "monkey," you should not be surprised when nature places you in a circumstance where you are rudely treated.

You must understand others just as eagerly as you would like to be understood, because it is by doing so that you prepare the karma of being understood. The world is a reflection of what you are. The way you act with people determines the way that the karmic reaction will unfold. If you promote understanding, you will be understood. If you promote misunderstanding, you will be misunderstood.

Spiritual virtues have a special magical quality. When you develop them within your personality, similar characteristics proceed from others and are directed towards you. If you are compassionate towards others, you will receive compassion from an external source in a time of need. If you do not have compassion, then you will not draw compassion from others.

So when the sincere urge to alleviate the sufferings of others blooms within your heart, in turn, you will obtain mercy. The entire Cosmic plan will show its mercy towards you because God is supremely merciful.

See Your Weaknesses Clearly

If a virtue is to be properly developed, one's unconscious must change. This takes great patience and self-introspection. If you fail in practicing a virtue, strive even harder to overcome your weaknesses. Try again and again, never to be daunted by failure.

Blindly asserting, "I am compassionate and I have always been so," does not allow you to practice benevolence, because you are not being reflective. It is only when you realize the ways in which you lack kindness that you can enthusiastically embrace the project of becoming compassionate. It is only when you know that you are not a good singer that you can become a better one.

So it is actually a great achievement to realize that you have only a limited degree of compassion. At the same time, you should have faith in the fact that compassion is an innate virtue of your soul. When the adventitious growth of cruelty is removed from your heart, you become the very embodiment of compassion and mercy.

Integrate Yourself to Better Serve Others

As long as your personality is imbalanced and eccentrically developed, the Divine quality of compassion cannot manifest in your thoughts and actions. In an imbalanced personality, the egoistic sentiment of attachment is mistaken for tender Divine Love, and selfish actions are mistaken for selfless service of humanity. Therefore, bring about integration and balance in your personality by the practice of a harmonious blend of wisdom, devotion, meditation and action in your daily life. Without integrating your personality properly and disciplining yourself, you will probably go off on tangents as you try to practice any virtue, and the chances are great that you will fail terribly.

Practicing Yoga to remove suffering from your own heart will allow you to understand the suffering in others from a more profound point of view. As you integrate yourself and root out the causes of misery within yourself, you become more qualified to understand people and their miseries, and you will be able to help them to a much greater extent by sharing your knowledge.

Rise beyond Ego

If a person has offended you, and you cling to your ego, whenever there is a threat, calamity, or adversity there will arise a deep-rooted despair that leaves you feeling helpless. You may wait to find an opportunity to offend the person equally or even with added interest. You might feel quite full of yourself at such a time; however, that feeling obstructs the perception of unity. It opposes your movement in expansion. And that type of movement intensifies ego, because for you to feel joyous about having hurt others, you must identify with your ego. The moment you understand the illusion of ego, there arises within you a sense of humiliation before your own eyes. You will realize, "I should not have stooped to that level."

In acts of true kindness and mercy, there is a transcendence of ego. However, such an amazing and transformative process is not easy. It is difficult to separate yourself even from ordinary physical things to which you are accustomed. It is far more challenging to be separated from the ego that you have been clinging to all your life.

If your mind begins to deeply appreciate qualities like compassion and begins to express them, you will spontaneously detach yourself from your ego. In the beginning, patience and endurance is required, often without any immediate reward. In fact, if you seek an external reward, then you have not understood virtue in the real sense. But gradually, as you persist with a deeper meditative process, you will realize that you have an eternal reward in the form of Cosmic expansion. As you increasingly loosen your identification with the ego, you are able to resolve all your problems. You are able to see your mental conflicts objectively and eventually realize that there are no problems. This is an advanced meaning of "Blessed are the merciful, for they shall obtain mercy."

See God behind the Mask of Wickedness

The teachings of Lord Jesus as well as those of Yoga philosophy and all true spiritual teachings emphasize that you continue to be kind despite the cruelty expressed towards you by others. Continue to be enduring while facing the opposition to goodness from others. Continue to maintain your deeper understanding of virtue undeterred by all external obstruction. If someone behaves spitefully towards you, it is easy to react with cruelty. However, greatness lies in controlling your own anger, and transforming that anger into love. If you do so, the cruel personality will eventually become transformed into a compassionate personality.

The moment a person is seen to have done something wrong or harmful, they are given the stamp of "criminal" or "undesirable." That is not the way a sincerely religious mind sees things. A merciful mind never sees a person as an absolute sinner. Cruelty and vices are diseases of the personality. A doctor does not hate the patient because the patient is ill. Rather, he helps remove the disease. In the same way, a Sage guides people to evolve spiritually rather than remaining focused on their narrow, limited mental conditions.

Therefore, as an aspirant, learn to see God as the underlying basis of all that exists. See God behind the mask of a wicked, violent and sinful personality. If you do so, it is possible that you will see the victory of love over hatred, and the victory of righteousness over unrighteousness.

When the impressions of anger, hatred, pride, fault-finding, cruelty and greed begin to dissolve due to the development of the positive impressions of love, compassion, humility, and generosity, then the inner stream of life begins to commune with universal life. Therefore, one becomes a fountain-source of inspiration to oneself, as well as to everyone else.

Exemplars of Divine Compassion

To develop true mercy or compassion, reeducate and transform your unconscious. This can be accomplished in various ways, but the most important method is *satsanga*, or good association. Keep your mind in constant association with the great ideals presented by Sages and Saints from all religions. Study their lives and understand how Divine qualities developed within their personalities and served as a blessing to others. Observe well how such advanced personalities behave towards their enemies, friends, and towards the obstacles in their lives. Sincere effort will give rise to compassion, which will emanate like fragrance from your blossoming heart. This fragrance of compassion will accelerate your path to Enlightenment and unity with God.

Lord Buddha and Lord Jesus are sublime embodiments of compassion. They lived only to relieve human beings of their deep-rooted maladies. Their acts of compassion and mercy belong not just to the period of time in which they existed, but to all humanity at all times.

Recall the powerful story of how Lord Jesus once encountered a lady surrounded by an angry crowd, judging her harshly for her sins:

> *They said to him, "Teacher, this woman has been caught in the act of adultery. Now, in the Law, Moses commanded us to stone such women. So what do you say?" This they said to test him that they might have some charge to bring against him. Jesus bent down and wrote with his finger on the ground. And as they continued to ask him, he stood up and said to them, "Let him who is without sin among you be the first to throw a stone at her." And once more he bent down and wrote on the ground. But when they heard*

it, they went away one by one, beginning
with the older ones, and Jesus was left alone
with the woman standing before him.
(KJV John 8: 4-9)

When Lord Buddha first saw misery, he began to reflect upon how misery could be eliminated. He worked on this problem until he attained Enlightenment or *Nirvana*. According to the story, one day the young Buddha, or Siddartha as he was then called, was out walking in the royal forest when he observed a hunter shoot a beautiful bird. He picked up the bird and saw that the arrow had pierced its body. Not knowing what pain was, he plucked out the arrow and plunged it into his own body. He felt miserable. Then he began to empathize with the bird.

At that time, the hunter ran over to Siddartha and said, "That's my bird! I shot it and I'm going to cook it. How dare you try to take it away from me!" Buddha responded, "I will not give you this bird no matter what you do." News of this reached his father, the king, and it was the king who ultimately decided that a person who saves life is better than one who takes it away. So in this way, Buddha was able to keep the bird. This is how Buddha's God-like compassion was kindled.

During his quest to eradicate suffering, Buddha practiced various austerities and teachings. Finally, through deep meditation, he eventually attained Enlightenment. He then reflected for a long period of time. Now that he had attained *Nirvana* and ended his own suffering, he thought that he would dissolve his physical body and remain immersed in the Bliss of *Nirvana* forever.

However, almost immediately after entertaining this thought, his compassionate heart asserted itself: "I have created a boat with great effort that has carried me across the stream of the world-process. Shouldn't I allow that boat to ferry other people across as well?" The moment that idea arose within his mind, Buddha refrained from dissolving his body. From that time on, he led a very active life, teaching others as his act of compassion.

The great Indian Sage, Valmiki, was a robber in his early days. Through the influence of great Sages, he transformed himself and became a devotee of Lord Rama. After a prolonged practice of devotion and *samadhi* (superconsciousness), he emerged as a totally different personality. One who had been so insensitive to others' miseries became so profoundly compassionate in his heart that when he saw a bird being separated from her mate by the cruel arrow of a hunter, he felt an upsurge of compassion. The outward event to him became a mirror reflecting the miseries of all living beings. Inspired by this Divine feeling, he composed the magnificent poetic work, the Ramayana, which abounds with amazing literary excellence, poetic sublimity and mystic insight.

If you have studied the Ramayana, you will recall that in this epic scripture, the monkeys and bears fought fiercely with the demons every day. After being crushed, miserably beaten up, and afflicted, they gathered in the ev ening before Lord Rama. Rama simply smiled at them with his magnanimous Divine compassion, and they were all miraculously healed.

The demons also felt crushed and battered by the day's end. But when they filed before Ravana, the demon king, he glared at them with his twenty eyes (Ravana had ten heads), making them feel even worse than before.

The secret of Rama's success was his compassion. Though he did not even so much as lay a hand on his monkey and bear warriors, the mere power of his compassionate gaze alleviated their suffering and left them feeling refreshed and renewed.

When great Saint Jnaneshwar was a boy, he was already well-established in the Vedantic vision of nonduality—the vision that all is the Self. One day the Saint saw several men beating a water buffalo. Noticing the Sage, they asked him whether he could feel the blows they were inflicting upon the water buffalo, since according to the Sage, the Self in the buffalo was the same as his very own Self. In response, Saint Jnaneshwar silently bared his back. The same stripes on the water buffalo's back had transferred to him by means of his intense feeling for the suffering animal. It is a most profound virtue to spontaneously feel the sufferings of others irrespective of their cast, creed, or national origin— human as well as nonhuman. Sage Jnaneshwar's empathy for the buffalo symbolizes this great Divine quality.

As we see in these exemplars of compassion as well as in the myriad of others who continue to bless our lives, the development of true compassion depends upon the revelation of the inner majesty of the Divine Self. Compassion or mercy is the fragrance emanating from the flower of Divine Love; it is not dependent upon any circumstantial development. Therefore, the compassion of a Sage is his very nature. Like moonlight radiating from the moon, a Sage radiates compassion in his surroundings and creates an atmosphere of harmony and peace. Although he may not be doing anything tangible or visible to most people, he is setting up a dynamic movement in the world just by his Divine and elevated feeling.

In the spiritual realm, there is a treasure that exists within your heart. That is the treasure of Divine virtues—and it includes the great gem of compassion or mercy. If you allow that treasure to reveal itself, it will enrich your soul abundantly. It is a treasure that can free you forever by carrying you to the state of Liberation; but if you have not awakened that treasure, you will continue to wander from birth to birth.

People exist as wanderers and beggars as long as they lack sufficient wealth for their basic needs. When they acquire wealth, however, they settle down and enjoy the security of a home. Similarly, the soul remains a wanderer as long as it does not have spiritual wealth. When it acquires that Divine treasure, it ceases to be a wanderer and enjoys the Bliss of the Self, one's Spiritual Home.

As long as your heart is filled with impressions of cruelty and gross indifference towards the miseries of others, you cannot enshrine God within it. Let your heart melt with the gentle rays of mercy and compassion, so that you may take flight from the prison of your personality and commune with the Universal Self!

VI. Blessed are the pure in heart, for they shall see God.

In this Beatitude, Christ promises the highest attainment of God-realization through purification of the heart, which in Yogic terminology is referred to as *chitta shuddhi*. Each religious tradition glorifies this attainment of Self-realization, though calling it by different names; and each recognizes the importance of purification on the path of spirituality.

The mind, like a mirror, reflects your own ever-present Divine Consciousness. However, impurities, agitations, and obstructions prevent that mirror of mind from revealing your Consciousness in all its perfection. *Sadhana* (the course of spiritual discipline chosen by an aspirant) is the mystical cleansing process that removes the impurities and obstructions and allows you to see the Self clearly reflected.

To better understand this role of *sadhana*, imagine that you are trying to see your face in a handheld mirror. If dust and dirt has gathered on the mirror, your face will appear distorted. Therefore, the pollutants of the mirror need to be removed. The dirt is like the gross contamination that colors the mind—anger, hated, greed, jealousy, pride, and similar defects. These gross impurities, referred to as *malas* in Yogic terminology, are washed away by Karma Yoga—consistently converting your actions into selfless service by considering yourself an instrument in Divine Hands.

Another obstacle to seeing your face in the mirror would result from an unsteady hand. If your hand is trembling with agitation, the image will also be distorted. These tremors are like the perpetual agitation inflicted upon the unenlightened mind due to restless, distracted, and externalized thought waves and desires. Such subtle impurities, referred to in Yogic terminology as *vikshepa*, are reduced and then eliminated by the patient practice of devotion and meditation.

The final obstacle to seeing your face in the mirror would be a veiling effect caused by your hair streaming down across your face. If you simply brush your hair away, with an easy movement, your face will clearly show itself. That veiling effect is like *avidya*, or ignorance of your true spiritual nature. By the practice of profound enquiry into "Who am I?" leading to the blossoming of intuitive intellect, you discover that the Divine Self shining in the mirror of your purified mind is your very Self.

Thus, throughout the course of *sadhana*, you must become increasingly aware of the crippling effect of the impure ego—that false "I" that asserts the feeling of *ahamta* (I-ness) and *mamata* (mineness). The ego gradually relaxes and is robbed of its power when you succeed in bringing God into every aspect of your life—performing your duties conscientiously, cultivating the treasure of Divine virtues, enjoying love of God, and succeeding in meditation and inquiry. As a result, your intellect ascertains the illusory nature of the ego, your heart opens completely to the majesty of the Divine Self and you are able to see that Self as the only Reality behind you and all that exists.

You Can See God!

Lord Jesus asserts, *"For they shall see God."* But does this mean that we can perceive God the way we perceive a candle flame, a table, chairs, a cake, or Christmas gifts? Can we touch God? Can we talk to God? Can God be seen? The fact is that God is not a form of speculation, but can be seen by the inner intuitive eye with a directness of perception that is unknown in the world of objects.

God can be seen directly, but the mind must first be purified. When the mind is purified intuition unfolds, linking itself to every sense within you. When you look into the sky with the naked eye you see nothing but a blue sky; but when you look through a telescope you see the vastness of space. Similarly, if you place before your eyes the telescope of intuitive vision, you will find God before you. Then you can touch God, you can see God, you can talk to God, you can walk with God, and you can become one with God. The Saints and Sages have given testimony to this fact. In all countries, Saints and Sages did not just philosophize about the existence of God; they actually had the awareness of oneness with God. Therefore, *"Blessed are the pure in heart"*—for they who have acquired that type of purity will have the vision of God.

In Vedantic teachings, seeing God—the ultimate blessing experienced by the pure in heart—is characterized by *brahmakara-vritti*: the unceasing, unimpeded flow of mind to God. Although an aspirant must exert considerable self-effort to succeed in *sadhana*, those efforts are all ultimately aimed at stilling the mind so that the effortless, intuitive revelation of the Self can spontaneously occur. In that stillness there blossoms a perpetual awareness of God as the only Reality behind all that exists.

Imagine, for a moment, that a lake in its agitation is trying to capture the sun by producing numerous waves. However, if the waves on the surface of the lake all shimmer so much in the light, the sun cannot be seen clearly in its entirety. When the lake reaches a higher state of wisdom, it realizes that creating more waves doesn't capture anything new. Therefore, it should just quiet the waves and remain still. The entire sun then majestically appears in the lake.

Similarly, the human heart longs to recapture its Oneness with God, but the agitation of the externalization of mind makes that impossible. As profound devotion and wisdom unfold through *sadhana*, mind discovers that the same Reality— *Brahman*, the Divine Self—is behind everything in this world of apparent multiplicity. Therefore, mind becomes placid and is no longer distracted by desires for objects and circumstances in the world of time and space. No longer is it obsessed with the question, "Which one should I pursue now?" Rather, the mind becomes internalized. It flows perpetually towards God through the highest mental function—*brahmakara-vritti*—and the glorious Light of the Self is revealed with perfect clarity.

Adorn Yourself with Divine Qualities

To see God as your own Self, you must ask yourself, "How can I be more like God?" What qualities does God possess that I can perfect in my own personality? A purified mind is one that is free from impressions of attachment, hatred, egoism, and selfishness. As long as these negative impressions exist, the unconscious will be a source of negative thoughts and the negative actions resulting from these thoughts. Therefore, the task before an aspirant is to replace these impure impressions with Divine impressions—impressions of humility, truthfulness, contentment, peace, harmony, and devotion that the Bhagavad Gita identifies as *daivi sampat*.

Conquering negative qualities within your personality is one of the greatest movements on the spiritual journey. The secret in sublimating lower tendencies lies in replacing them with their positive counterparts. For instance, if you are feeling hatred, gradually develop the quality of love. If you are struggling with anger, patiently promote forgiveness or compassion. In this way you attain greater purity or *sattwa* within your personality. *Sattwa* is one of the three modes of nature that constantly condition your mind. *Rajas* (restless externalization and ostentatiousness) and *tamas* (dullness and inertia) are the other two. You can transmute *rajas* and *tamas* into *sattwa* by training your mind to perform righteous actions through thought, word, and deed, and by patiently cultivating Divine virtues (*daivi sampat*). When your personality becomes perfectly adorned with those jewels of virtue, you will see God. To see God or to know God means to become God.

The Secret to Unlocking Your Divine Potential

Beyond the level of conscious thought there exists a vast realm of mind known as the unconscious. The mind that everyone is aware of is only a tiny fragment of the massive mind. It is like the tip of an iceberg—what you see is small and what you don't see can capsize a ship. The portion of the mind that is hidden in the unconscious holds the mystery of one's life. The potential, progress and evolution of a person are all related to the unconscious. In every lifetime one touches only a small portion of that mind, sometimes utilizing it, sometimes misusing it. It is necessary to gain an understanding of the subtler realms of mind in order to rise above the influences of the lower self and mold one's character and destiny according to will and reason. The movement towards God, in a philosophical sense, is the movement towards the root and the center of one's being. Therefore, removal of the unconscious complexes is the direct means to God-realization or Self-realization. The roots of human thoughts and feelings are embedded in the unconscious. Therefore, unless the unconscious is explored and its subtle desires, complexes and frustrations are sublimated and transformed, it is not possible for anyone to succeed on the path to Liberation.

The unconscious mind, once purified, enables you to develop excellent qualities in your personality. Conversely, when your unconscious is impure and uncultured, you develop negative qualities and habits in your personality and morbid thoughts and sentiments become dominant. By elevating your unconscious, you discover the endless glories of the soul; on the other hand, by degrading your unconscious, you continue to move down the steps of the spiritual ladder like a ball falling down a staircase.

No matter how much wealth you may possess, if your unconscious is laden with negative impressions, you cannot feel the free flow of life pulsating through your veins. Though seated in the midst of the most enchanting sights of nature, you will feel deep within yourself as if you are confined in a prison cell.

Therefore, culture of the unconscious is real culture, and education of the unconscious is real education. The greater part of your being is hidden in your unconscious. If you are able to release the impurities of the unconscious and unfold its latent powers, you will be the possessor of a mighty personality—a personality that pulsates with life and moves with success, a personality that becomes the channel of Divine Will and through it manifests beauty, grace, sublime ideals, and Divine activities.

Good Association Is a Powerful Force for Purifying the Heart

The uplifting atmosphere of *satsanga* (good association) is a powerful method of charging and elevating the unconscious with spiritual vibrations. Generally, such *satsanga* is characterized by a group of sincere aspirants listening to a spiritual discourse by an enlightened Guru. However, any book that elevates your mind, any action that instills joy and inspiration within you, and any company that aids your moral and spiritual growth is *satsanga*. If your life is filled with good association, if you hear the sublime lessons of life through spiritual teachers, if you endeavor to keep your mind tranquil, and if you practice meditation and reflection, then your efforts will feed the unconscious with positive vibrations that destroy embedded negative impressions. Every complex that exists in the unconscious mind puts a pressure on your life and imprisons your willpower to a certain extent. But when positive vibrations sweep over the inner realms of the unconscious, the complexes wither away and the imprisoned powers are released, just as fragrance escapes from blooming buds.

Your unconscious mind imitates others' behavior and opinions like a monkey. If you place yourself in the company of a person whose mind is filled with fear and insecurity, you will develop these traits unknowingly. Similarly, if you place yourself in the company of a Sage whose personality radiates Divine Love, understanding, and spiritual strength, you will begin to discover exalted qualities within yourself. The elevated unconscious of a Sage exerts a benevolent influence on the unconscious of a disciple. Just as water spills from a higher level to a lower level, so too, spiritual influence cascades from an elevated mind to a less elevated mind.

There is an ancient Indian parable in which Sage Narada experiences the greatness of *satsanga*. Narada became eager to hear about the glory of *satsanga* and so he decided to ask the greatest authority— Lord Vishnu. Unfortunately, Lord Vishnu said he was too busy at the moment to give such a serious matter an adequate reply. However, he told Narada to go into the forest and find a certain squirrel in a giant tree who would expound on the wonderful attributes of *satsanga*. Narada was puzzled. He wondered how a squirrel could tell him about such a subject. However, since you cannot argue with God, Narada followed Lord Vishnu's instructions and went to the forest.

It was early morning. The mist had lifted and the rays of the sun had warmed the forest. A little squirrel was there, jumping up and down and cracking nuts in the tree. Narada looked up and asked the squirrel if he would please give him insight into the glory of *satsanga*. The squirrel gazed intensely at Narada then suddenly fell from the tree and died. Narada was shocked and felt great sympathy towards that tender little creature. He returned to Vishnu and said, "Oh Lord, I could not receive any teachings about *satsanga* from the squirrel. He died before answering my request."

Lord Vishnu responded, "I still do not have time to give you an explanation, but please return to that same tree. This time, you will find a monkey who will relate to you the wondrous attributes of *satsanga*. Narada was not very enthusiastic about being instructed by a monkey. Nevertheless, again he went to that particular tree in the forest, looked up and found a monkey playfully bouncing from branch to branch, making strange sounds. Narada told the monkey he had been sent by Lord Vishnu to ask him about the glory of *satsanga*. The monkey immediately became very calm and serious; all his limbs relaxed. Narada eagerly waited to hear what the monkey had to tell him, but suddenly the lifeless body of the monkey fell at his feet.

Narada's heart sunk. Again he returned and waited for an occasion to meet Lord Vishnu. After Lord Vishnu heard his story, he said, "Oh Narada, go to a certain country where a prince was recently born to the royal family. There ask that newborn child to describe to you the glorious qualities of *satsanga*." Narada was quite worried. It was bad enough when the little creatures of the forest died, but it would be terrible if the prince were to pass on when Narada asked him about *satsanga*. However, Narada, trusting Lord Vishnu, followed his instructions. Upon reaching the palace, the king was very pleased to see Narada and asked him to confer his blessings on the newborn child. Narada said that this was the purpose of his visit, but asked to be alone with the child. The king agreed.

Finding the newborn prince by himself, Narada approached the child and told him with a trembling heart that Lord Vishnu had sent him to learn about the glory of *satsanga*. The child's eyes focused and his body became still. Narada's heart nearly stopped. Suddenly, the child began to speak: "Oh Narada, don't you realize that it was by your *satsanga* that the squirrel left its embodiment to become a monkey and then left its monkey embodiment to become a prince? Moreover, I was the squirrel, the monkey and now the royal prince, all due to the transformative power of your *satsanga*!"

The subtle meaning behind this story applies to everyone. In every personality, there is a squirrel that hoards and cracks nuts. When you practice *satsanga*, that "squirrel" dies. The aspect of your personality that accumulates and stores anger, hate, greed, irrational tensions and fear fades when you enjoy *satsanga*. That is the destruction of *mala* (gross impurities). The next obstacle you encounter is *vikshepa* (distraction)—the monkey state. The moment you destroy the lowest squirrel-aspect of your personality, you discover that the mind is filled with abundant energy, jumping constantly and swinging like a monkey from branch to branch. However, the force of *satsanga* sublimates that distraction as well. *Sattwa* or purity then fills the mind. Through that elevated mind you realize you are not an individual dependent on objects. You are the ruler of all that exists, the emperor of emperors. So, from a squirrel-like personality, led by *satsanga*, you attain a princely personality.

Satsanga is the most potent remedy for all troubles that assail human beings. Poverty, disease, calamities and death—all these invade the mind. However, when you nourish your mind with the nectar of *satsanga*, when the mind has discovered the Truth and perceives the eternity of the Self, then sorrow disappears. The sorrowful world becomes a dream. Calamities become like drifting clouds that cannot hurt the sky. Discover the power of the potent remedy of *satsanga* and how its miraculous healing powers can purify your heart and change your life.

Powerful methods for cultivating the unconscious mind can be introduced into your life every single day. Do not waste a moment in securing the intuitive vision of your own true Self! Christ's teachings in the Beatitudes outline the journey of all religious aspirants towards purity of heart—*chitta shuddhi*. Once you have cleaned the mirror of your mind, it is able to perfectly reflect your Divine Consciousness within. That Consciousness is ever present, waiting to be revealed to your inner eye. Blessed are the pure for they see God as their very own Self.

VII. Blessed are the peacemakers, for they shall be called Children of God.

Throughout human history, much has been said about promoting peace in the world. Religious reformers have come and gone. Political leaders have exercised their powers in various ways. Saints, Sages, and Divine incarnations have again and again emphasized the need for righteousness and virtue. The world, however, continues to be filled with tension and discord. A religious teacher once said in jest, "The world is like a dog's tail—you straighten it, and it curls back again." It is necessary, therefore, to reflect more deeply upon this problem of promoting peace with the help of profound spiritual philosophy and enlightened teachings.

According to Yoga (Vedanta) philosophy, the world of time and space is a relative existence. It is not reality in the absolute sense. It is *Maya* (illusion). Even in the light of scientific discoveries, the world is shown to be a phenomenon of relativity and appearance. With closer observation, it is clear that every individual sees the world in his own particular way. Though the physical world continues to hold a standard of reality for all human beings, the psychological world continues to differ from one individual to another. Your mental experiences are defined by your likes and dislikes, your expectations and their fulfillment, your relationships and identifications. Therefore, the world is not the same for everyone. To a thief, the world seems to be filled with thieves; to a person overcome by sorrow, the radiant moon pours down a stream of agony; and for a person of mystic understanding, the world is experienced as a manifestation of the Divine Self, as a surging ocean of joy.

The world that constantly challenges you to struggle is not so much the outer, geographical world. Rather, it is the inner world based upon the unconscious structure of the mind, and the conscious reactions to the circumstances that exist outside. Therefore, if you are to experience peace and joy, you must make a profound adjustment within yourself. The problem of world peace cannot be encountered in the outer world. It dwells in the human heart, where it must be tackled, confronted and resolved.

Yoga philosophy proclaims that the innermost reality of man is not individual but cosmic. Deep within your heart lies your true identity. What you think you are is not really who you are. Christ told His disciples, *"I and the Father are One"* and *"The Kingdom of Heaven is within thee."* In the Old Testament of the Bible, Moses asked God, *"What is your name?"* And God answered, *"I am That am I."* That "I am" is an internal awareness of God's presence in your heart. In other words, your real identity is the Divine Self or *Brahman*. You are essentially One with God. That Self that underlies your personality also underlies the personalities of all other living beings and, indeed, the entire world-process.

Deep down we all have an innate yearning to discover unity in existence and our unity with God. No matter how long it takes, no matter how many embodiments we may have, the final destination for the soul is the discovery that, "I am one with the Divine Self." Like rivers blending with the ocean, all souls must merge in God.

This knowledge of *Brahman* must not remain merely on the level of intellectual knowledge, but rather must be glimpsed and finally realized by intuition. Mere intellectual knowledge gives rise to a superficial state of peacefulness, while one's heart continues to harbor subtle roots of anger, hate, greed and passion. Therefore, mere intellectual knowledge continues to create disharmony and discord within one's personality as well as outside of oneself, because it cannot eradicate the roots of impurities. On the other hand, intuitional knowledge eradicates those impurities and fills one's heart with the fragrance of Heaven in the form of Divine virtues.

As you succeed in kindling the light of intuition, it enables you to enjoy higher levels of personality integration and to undergo a process of genuine transformation. It is this light that enables you to truly understand yourself and the world in which you live. In the process of spiritual awakening, with the unfolding of intuition, you discover within yourself the nectarine stream of universal unity. And this discovery is the solution to all problems of the world and a key to abounding world peace.

Mankind must strive to stop chasing the mirage of individuality, seeking happiness in the world through the products of illusion. People continue to keep their minds confined to values based upon an ego-dominated reason. They continue to be identified with what they are not, and try to quench their thirst for peace and bliss in sparkling waters of a mirage. Instead of realizing the universal unity of life, they continue to assert themselves as individuals, interpreting their successes and failures in the language of the limited mind.

It is this faulty movement in ignorance that fills the human heart with morbid sentiments. Instead of the sublime sentiment of universal love, people develop love ruled by ego; and such love fans the smoke of violence, greed, hatred, passion, and manifold perversions in their personalities. Without a center deeper than their ego, they will be unable to develop courage during adversity; they will find themselves helpless when their temper overpowers their mind like a raging storm; and they will remain confounded when confronted with frustrating conditions of life and diverse circumstances caused by human relationships.

On the other hand, if the human heart were filled with the vision of truth, people would possess the most sublime qualities of the head and heart. It would be impossible for them to cause disharmony in the world. Rather they would be a source of higher ideals that promote peace and understanding and remove the sufferings and sorrows of mankind. They would become true Children of God.

As Children of God, brothers and sisters may have their quarrels, yet they are always bonded together by the strings of Love. Their Divine bond eases difficult situations and reminds them that their relationship is at a deeper level, and that the world is an extension of their own Self. Such a great ideal is propagated by all religious traditions, and if everyone were to understand that ideal profoundly, world peace would not be out of reach.

Peace Begins within You

Your spiritual movement inward is not limited to your own personality; it always has its outer expression. If you bring peace within yourself, you will become a peacemaker in the world outside. But without finding peace within yourself, or without at least having the ideal of finding peace within, you could not bring peace to the world.

Being too enthusiastic about bringing peace to the world without first finding inner peace within yourself will bring immense stress and distraction within your own mind, and may actually create havoc around you. Universal Love cannot be kindled through a sentimental process. If, in trying to love everyone, you become so ecstatic that you forget about doing your duties at home or even at work, then that isn't universal Love—it's just sentimentality.

It is not easy to establish peace in the world, or even in people who are inimical towards each other. Even in ordinary circumstances, to bring about peace anywhere requires a mind that can perceive contending parties in a calm and detached manner. Such detachment is only possible when one's mind has become highly advanced and deeply peaceful itself.

You become a true peacemaker when you discover God within yourself and understand Him to be the underlying reality behind the world. Then when you perform your duties for human beings, when you serve your family, friends, and society at large, you are loving God within them.

As peace grows within your own heart, you realize that all human beings are expressions of God; all are media for God's Presence. God comes to each of us through both enemies and friends. If He comes as an enemy, it is a greater challenge to love Him. Seeing the Self in all does not mean that practical realities should be ignored. You must always do your utmost to protect yourself from harm. However, if you see your Self in all, you cannot easily become violent, and the world will become a more peaceful place because of it.

When you view your actions in this light, impressions of attachment and hatred do not easily arise. As you push away attachment and hatred, you transcend your ego and discover true universal love. This enables you to serve one and all with an ever-increasing depth of wisdom and compassion. And the more people who love and serve others in this way, the more peace will flourish in the world.

As you move towards a deep realization of unity within yourself, your personality resembles a blossoming flower emanating fragrance. In every movement, you express something unique that catches the imagination and the sensitivity of others. Even though you may not say anything about your techniques and experiences, your personality creates an indelible impression upon the minds of others according to their sensitivity. As your own consciousness expands and you enjoy increasing mental purity, you experience a love that is universal and Divine. Automatically your personality radiates that love—and there is no way to stop it!

In the physical world an outburst of energy anywhere exerts a subtle influence on distant parts of the world. An atomic bomb may be exploded in a remote desert, yet its manifold effects may be seen everywhere. In the same manner, there is an amazing outburst of spiritual energy when you "sacrifice" your worldly intellect at the altar of intuitional knowledge, when you give up hatred for the sake of experiencing profound love, when you overpower pride for the sake of humility, and when you crucify your very ego for the sake of union with God. Unlike the devastating effects of atomic explosions, this outburst of spiritual energy radiates uplifting, elevating and inspiring vibrations for centuries to come, and countless souls, touched by those vibrations, become blessed.

Sages and Saints—The Ideal Children of God

It is by Self-realization alone that one is able to truly resolve the root of all problems within the heart and, in turn, become a channel of the sublime actions, thoughts and insights that are most effective in promoting peace and harmony in the world. Therefore, enlightened Sages and Saints are indeed the most perfect Children of God.

They enjoy the Peace of the Self—the peace that "passeth all understanding." They are the fountain source of harmony for the world. In them the howling waves of negative thoughts are silenced, the very storm of the mind is stilled as the soul seeks its communion with God in transcendental silence. Self-realized personalities live to bring love where there is hate, clarity where there is confusion, understanding where there is quarrel and tension, joy where there is sorrow, harmony where there is discord and dissension, and light where there is darkness.

Every living being is a Sage-not-yet-come. With Enlightenment, you truly understand the Upanishadic declaration: *"Ayam Atma Shanto"*—"I am the very embodiment of Peace." With Enlightenment, you become as perfect as your Father in Heaven and you inherit His Divine Kingdom—the Kingdom of Heaven. Like Lord Jesus, the Son of God, you become a perfect Child of God, a perfect peacemaker.

VIII. Blessed are they that are persecuted for righteousness' sake, for theirs is the Kingdom of Heaven. For, blessed are you, when men shall revile you, and persecute you, and shall say all manner of evil against you falsely, for my sake. Rejoice, and be exceeding glad, for great is your reward in Heaven, for so persecuted they the prophets which were before you.

The path of righteousness is never adorned only with roses; it must have innumerable thorns as well. When great Saints begin to spread their wisdom among the masses, they are often opposed and condemned, for the standard of virtue of the masses is fickle in nature. It changes with one's mood, fluctuates according to the dictates of ego, swings with variations in the social and political climate in which one lives. Thus, a spiritual seeker, in pursuing a course of action, must not be inclined merely to

satisfy the mass mentality, but rather to be true to the deeper Self.

It is often seen that a saintly person is respected by others as a symbol of virtue only as long as his actions agree with their limited understanding and lesser values. But when one advances on the path of Truth, respect is often replaced by animosity, insults, and resistance. This can be clearly seen in the life of Buddha.

On the path to attaining *Nirvana*, Buddha adopted a very severe method that he thought would help bring about Self-realization. Because of his extreme austerity he had attracted a group of seven disciples who decided to join him. These new disciples saw how this once wealthy prince now lived in such a ragged state within the forest, enduring the heat and cold, and possessing nothing. They thought, "Here is a man who had everything and has renounced it all. We should follow him."

As time went by, Buddha suffered from extreme weakness due to fasting, causing him to remain unconscious for several days. During this time his disciples thought, "How wonderful, he is in *samadhi*!" And they were all eagerly expecting him to become Buddha the Enlightened, hoping they would receive the first blessings from the realized Sage. In the meantime, they eagerly went to the village and begged to receive plenty of food to keep themselves strong. However, they would not envision Buddha eating food and living in even the slightest comfort.

Soon Buddha realized that he couldn't advance in meditation and *samadhi* and attain his spiritual goal in his weakened physical condition. So he mentally willed that he should have food to sustain his body. The moment he willed this, he was approached by a village lady known as Sujata. She was a farmer's wife who had vowed that if she were blessed with a son she would come to that forest and worship the forest deity. That was precisely the time when her wishes were fulfilled, so she brought a richly prepared rice pudding on a golden platter to be presented to the forest god. But finding that there was no other godly being but Buddha, she thought, "Why not worship a living god rather than wait for an invisible one." She also thought, "Maybe the forest god has assumed this form." So she presented the food before him and Buddha immediately said, "I am not the god whom you wanted to worship. Nevertheless, I am hungry." Hearing his words, Sujata allowed Buddha to eat the pudding. As he ate the food, she fanned him with great feeling and devotion. When the seven disciples returned and saw from a distance what was happening, they thought Buddha was caught in illusion and was entangled in the grip of *Maya*. As a result, they all immediately abandoned him.

As this episode in Buddha's life reveals, as you begin to advance in spiritual profundity, those who once revered you may begin to criticize and insult you due to lack of understanding. Unfortunately, there is often a psychological demand among fellow aspirants, family members, friends and colleagues in the world that you should not advance more than they do. Therefore, there arises the urge to draw you back, to pull your legs. When this occurs your mind must be ready to see that even the fondest friend or relative may become an enemy.

However, even if you are persecuted due to misunderstanding, you must continue steadfastly to pursue Truth according to your own ethical standards. As you continue to progress naturally according to the path of *sadhana* you have chosen, there arises an "escape velocity" that makes it impossible for others to pull you back. If you are on the right path, you must continue, even if the whole world opposes you. If your suffering is for the sake of righteousness, the Divine Self will endow your personality with unimaginable strength and courage.

If the masses do not appreciate his expressions or activities, a Sage is not bothered by it at all. And thus he finds himself alone—not with loneliness but with God, endowed with tremendous force to carry out the particular movement that he has adopted. That has been the example of Sages from all times.

Christ allowed Himself to be crucified. He could have sought the advice of more experienced people and found a way to avoid being captured. Socrates could have escaped from prison, since there were many people ready to bribe the prison attendants to release him; but Socrates decided he would rather drink the poison than abandon his adherence to Truth. Mahatma Gandhi lived a life of intense austerity, ever ready to die for his righteous goals.

Learning the art of standing up for righteousness, standing up for what you believe in, has been the message of all great leaders and Saints and Sages alike. This art strengthens your fortitude and resolve to adhere to what your own soul is guiding you to do. And interestingly enough, although the virtuous actions of a saintly personality are not meant to please others, they eventually do become pleasing to people of every age. There is a special sweetness exuded by suffering for righteousness' sake—and eventually all the forces that were against a righteous person turn in their favor.

The Sublime Nobility of Suffering

A spiritual aspirant lives a life pervaded by a sense of sacrifice. With a Godward vision, adversities are converted into austerities, and persecutions offered by the world are converted into a process of self-purification. Thus an aspirant sacrifices his grosser qualities for the emergence of the subtler qualities of the soul. Just as gold shines when melted, the spirit of an aspirant shines when it is persecuted for the sake of righteousness.

The blazing movement towards the limitless Self is obstructed by the dark clouds of the world of limitation. However, the resistance offered on the path of an aspirant quickens his steps towards the final goal, instead of obstructing him. Simultaneously, this devotee of God sees sweetness in suffering for the Divine Self. With the increasing experience of Divine sweetness, it becomes impossible to return hated for hated, violence for violence, and cruelty for cruelty.

When you become aware of the fact that all that you suffer and endure is for the promotion of righteousness, for the sake of God Himself, then you accept your sufferings as blessings from God. When you suffer for the sake of someone whom you love intensely, there is sweetness behind that suffering. When God becomes that object of your love and you understand that your entire life is a movement towards God-realization, all your sufferings become sweet. So when you are reviled, when you are insulted, when bitter words are spoken against you, you remain calm and composed, enjoying inner peace and serenity. Instead of drawing bitter impressions from the world, you begin to draw from within yourself a sweet awareness of Divine Presence and an understanding that you are worshiping God in all that you do.

When you are persecuted for the sake of righteousness, there is a sense of heroism within your mind, a purpose for which you are suffering. The masses suffer without any purpose, simply feeling the pain of certain difficult situations and circumstances in life. But when you suffer as an aspirant, it has a purpose. You understand that there is a mystic insight to be gained and as a result your feelings become sublime rather than degraded. Therefore, your suffering is not suffering at all.

Both the Eastern and Western scriptures abound with examples of how God suffers for the benefit of humanity. The Christian religion teaches how Christ accepted the Cross because of the immense love He had for humanity and how His death and resurrection absolved the faithful of all sins. In the light of Vedanta, this implies that Christ has already destroyed all of the demoniac qualities within your personality and has paved the way for your purity leading to God-realization.

Similarly, in Hindu scriptures, Lord Shiva is mystically portrayed as *neela kantha*—possessing a blue throat. The story tells how once upon a time the milky ocean was churned and during the churning process poison emerged. No one was powerful enough to consume it except for Lord Shiva, who drank this poison and held it in his throat for the greater good of the world. The ocean refers to the unconscious mind. The path of *sadhana* is like a churning process, and out of it emerges nectar— symbolizing virtuous qualities, as well as poison— representing demoniac qualities. When you advance in *sadhana* on the spiritual path, you realize that you have the same strength as Shiva and are able to handle the various negative manifestations within and transform all of them into Divine qualities that beautify your personality.

At the highest level all sins and impurities have already been destroyed by God Himself. This idea instills great faith in your mind as it leads you to feel God's presence and support in your spiritual movement. Essentially the Self is untouched, unscathed, and ever pure. The impurities you find within yourself come from the veil of illusion that tells you, "I am this body-mind complex." Once you begin to understand Who you are, you realize that there is neither one who can sin nor one who can be persecuted, since the Self is beyond these concepts of the mind.

The trials, tribulations and sufferings that you endure on the path of righteousness are blessings in themselves. St. Peter says in his epistle,

God will bless you, even if others treat you unfairly for being loyal to him. You don't gain anything by being punished for some wrong you have done. But God will bless you, if you have to suffer for doing something good. After all, God chose you to suffer as you follow in the footsteps of Christ, who set an example by suffering for you.
(CEV 1 Peter 2: 19-21)

Every time you suffer for a righteous cause, each time you face tribulation for promoting peace, every time you sacrifice for the good of others, you are drawn closer and closer to God. The strength that you experience in combating against your difficult circumstances is an indication of the fact that God is drawing you to Himself. Thus, through prayer and internal resignation, you draw spiritual strength from God, which in turn allows you to be firm and undaunted even in the face of the bitterest situations in life.

Urging His followers to remain unaffected by trials and tribulations, Lord Jesus said in the Sermon on the Mount:

Rejoice and be exceedingly glad,
for great is your reward in Heaven,
for so they persecuted the prophets
who were before you.

Jesus taught that if one faces persecutions or adversities with the Kingdom of Heaven as his goal, he will rejoice. If the Kingdom of Heaven is not one's main goal, then even in prosperous situations one will be miserable.

Why should one rejoice in the face of adversity? This is a very important spiritual point to be reflected upon and understood. In adverse situations your ego is being challenged—and that challenge is essential for genuine spiritual evolution. Human beings cling to their egos so tenaciously that they cannot let go of the ego unless they are thoroughly frustrated by life. Although you may have heard about the Kingdom of Heaven, and you may have even glimpsed the majesty of being One with the universal Self, still your ego stands in the way as a tremendous barrier.

In daily life your mind is constantly dominated by the voices of the ego. In the early morning you meditate, "I and God are One. The Kingdom of Heaven is within me." You then open the door and start mingling with people. Immediately, someone does not say "good morning" to you; someone does not give you the right type of appreciation. You are thrown off your rootedness in the Universal Life. Sometimes events are insignificant and sometimes they are major. Yet, according to Lord Jesus, all major events are insignificant. When something jars your ego, you begin to understand how your ego can be an obstacle, and that your task is to sublimate it. Thus, you learn to consider every jarring situation as a blessing.

It is similar to having a splinter lodged somewhere in your body, which only becomes evident when it is pressed. The pinch you feel reminds you of the need to remove it. Therefore, it is a blessing when someone gives your ego a pinch; it tells you where the thorn is.

The moment you understand that you are living to transform your ego, living to transcend the world of relativity and plunge into the Universal Self, you will begin to rejoice. It should therefore become your project to soar wholeheartedly into the transcendental realm. Each time someone provokes your ego, rejoice. Every time there is an adversity, rejoice. The ideal before you is to enjoy communion with God even in jarring situations, not only when you are seated in meditation. Keep that ideal in view, and rejoice.

When you follow this project of transcending the ego, you begin to discover the Light of your soul—which has been veiled by the ego. Referring to this most inspiring discovery, Lord Jesus said:

> *Let your light so shine before men, that they may see your good works, and glorify your Father which is in Heaven.*
> (KJV Matthew 5:16)

Chapter Seven

Take Up the Cross and Follow Me

The entire mysticism of Christ's teachings can be summed up in the ancient symbol of the Cross, which is also an important part of Vedic symbolism. In the Cross, a vertical line intersects a horizontal line.

The horizontal line symbolizes vision that is caught up in the world of the mind and senses, the world of relativity, the world of names and forms, the world of material ambitions, the world of illusion, infatuation and bondage. To be involved in the world is to follow the path of *preya*—the pleasant, which continues to keep the soul entangled in the world-process.

When your mind is constantly thinking of the past, struggling to face present situations, and planning for the future, it is working horizontally. On the horizontal plane, you are constantly pressured by karmas. While steadily unloading karmas with the left hand, you continue loading more with the right.

In exasperation, people cry, "When will I have time for prayer? When will I have time for meditation?" That is the great puzzle. How does one live in a world of inescapable responsibilities that will not allow you a moment of peace, and still be able to approach God?

The secret to approaching God reveals itself in the vertical line of the Cross. Through the Cross, Lord Jesus mystically teaches us to develop the vertical vision that intercepts the horizontal timeline of past, present and future and soar into the realm of the transcendental. It is a movement through the mind and intellect towards intuition, wherein the human soul merges with God.

When your mind turns towards God, it is functioning in a vertical direction. The vertical line points to the transcendence of the world of time and space, to the recognition of the world of the spirit. It is indicative of the path of *shreya*—the path of blessedness, which leads to Liberation.

With vertical vision you develop an awareness that true happiness is not in the past or future. It is not in material ambition, but in spiritual aspiration. True happiness is deep within your heart, where time and space are left behind. The Upanishadic teaching of "*Neti-Neti*"—"Not this, Not this," is the recognition that the path of the body, mind, senses and ego are ultimately not the path to that Supreme

Joy of the Self. The spiritual movement leads you to the glorious state of Pure Consciousness, wherein the little self is utterly negated in exchange for the Kingdom of Heaven.

The vertical line represents the vision of love that enables one to see all living beings in the light of God. The whole of creation is simply a vast temple that God has placed you in, and He has given you the ability and opportunity to serve and adore Him in an infinite number of ways. Therefore, if love of God has blossomed within your heart, and if you are filled with the awareness that Divinity is the essence of all, then you become worthy of Lord Jesus. And it is for that goal that Lord Jesus and other great incarnations such as Rama, Krishna, and Buddha came with the same profound message: to detach from the world and attach to God. Detach and attach. This is the subtle secret of all religions.

The great spiritual art to be learned is how to break free of the relative consciousness that repeatedly draws you into the captivating world of time and space. In order to do so, we must, according to Lord Jesus, develop a single vision or a single eye. To have a single eye implies that your mind understands that God is the only reality behind everything; there is nothing else. The transcendental alone exists, permeating all.

A human being is like a wave, unaware that its underlying reality is the ocean, the Cosmic Reality. This is again and again indicated by all religions of the world. When Moses asked God His name, the Divine voice said, *"I Am That Am I,"* which is a translation of *"Soham Asmi."* That "I Am" in you that transcends the limited human ego is the eternal Self. If that understanding is developed through prayer and reflection, you will attain perfection— the vertical vision.

Let Your Eye Be Single

No one, after lighting a lamp, puts it away in a cellar nor under a basket, but on the lamp stand, so that those who enter may see the light. The eye is the lamp of your body; when your eye is clear, your whole body also is full of light; but when it is bad, your body also is full of darkness. Then watch out that the light in you is not darkness.
(Luke 11:33-35)

If your egoistic (or horizontal) vision were to be transcended, you would discover that the Divine Vision, God's eye, is the Reality within you. It is the vertical axis, the single eye. The vertical axis refers to the intuitional mind. When the intuitional mind transcends the senses and the ego, the horizontal plane of the Cross, it perceives nonduality. God alone is real; there is nothing else. If that vision dawns within you, then you are filled with Light. You possess the Body of Light, not the physical body that perishes. You become eternal spirit, one with God.

Lord Jesus says that if you do not have that single eye, you have the eye of darkness or dualistic vision that becomes the basis for trouble. Such vision creates difficulties because it blocks your awareness of God. Dualistic vision implies that on the one hand you want God to comfort you, and on the other hand you hold onto the world. You believe that if God fails, the world will support you, and if the world fails, then God will provide a support. There is an inherent misunderstanding in this view.

When you realize that God is like the ocean, encompassing all that is, then there is no need to think of God and the world as two different things. If you have God, the world is automatically included. If you have the ocean, the waves are automatically incorporated. As the mind advances, it doesn't see duality; it doesn't perceive differences. It sees the Divine Self as the only Reality, the fundamental essence of the entire universe.

To understand the concept of vertical movement more clearly, reflect upon deep sleep, where time and space are transcended. The ego is transcended and you are free of all worries, anxieties, and even dreams. But deep sleep occurs according to nature's compulsion. How wonderful it would be if you could unburden your mind so that even while awake, handling the various problems of the world, your mind remained relaxed and flowed towards the Divine Self! A feeling of closeness to God and a sweet sense of surrender to the Divine Will constitute the Godward or vertical movement of the mind, intercepting the horizontal world of time and space.

The moment you begin to enjoy that vertical ascension, it becomes clear that you should be very careful not to become overly involved with the world. Whenever you react or use harsh words and display bitterness, you become immersed in the sticky substance of the world, and it is difficult to pull yourself out of the glue. Your mind continues to dwell upon the burden of the world. The art is to live your life with such adaptability and wisdom that while completing your duties you can remain relaxed. In the midst of activities, your mind does not lose sight of the Divine Presence. Then it is possible to enjoy serenity, which shines brighter than gold or any diamond.

If you were to "take up the Cross" and follow Christ in your daily life, you would be promoting peace and harmony within yourself, as well as rendering a dynamic service towards the spiritual progress of humanity—a form of progress that is more real and tangible than mere materialistic progress. Humanity must therefore harken to the message of the Cross in order to solve its numerous problems and enjoy the boundless blessings of its Divine potentiality.

Chapter Eight

The Kingdom of Heaven Is Within Thee

The terms "Heaven" and "Hell" have had great importance in human society and in the teachings of Christianity over the ages. Many people consider Heaven or Hell to be planes of existence that one experiences after death according to how good or evil their actions have been while they were alive. In the Vedic tradition, Heaven and Hell play a similar role in the context of astral experience after death. However, in both the teachings of Lord Jesus and in those of enlightened Sages, Heaven and Hell take on a more profound meaning and significance.

On a more abstract level, we can consider Hell to be separation from God, while Heaven is abiding in God. Selfishness, pride, greed, lust, violence, hatred, jealousy, hypocrisy and other mental impurities arise from the negation of the Divine Presence in human heart. These lead one to a hellish experience characterized by increasing pain and sorrow. On the other hand, truthfulness, humility, compassion, non-covetousness, generosity, fearlessness, cheerfulness and other virtues arise from the affirmation of Divine Presence within one's heart. These lead to a heavenly experience of increasing peace and joy. These heavenly and hellish experiences are known to all, even while they are alive on earth.

On the highest level of understanding, when Lord Jesus so magnificently asserts, *"The Kingdom of Heaven is within thee,"* He is speaking about the one goal of all religions: God-realization, Enlightenment or *Nirvana.* This powerful statement of Lord Jesus is explicit in pointing out that the Heaven you seek is not outside of yourself and not to be expected as a future event; rather, it is the intrinsic fact of your existence. You must seek Heaven through an inner transformation.

The same theme reverberates in such great utterances of Vedanta as *"Thou Art That."* With these words, the Guru instructs the disciple: You are not this passing personality or any of the limited concepts that you, in ignorance, consider yourself to be. Through purification of mind you will discover that you are that Pure Consciousness that is the Essence of all. You are *Brahman,* the Supreme Self. To Lord Jesus, God is identical with Heaven. Therefore, abiding in Heaven is the same as abiding

in God. This is described in Vedanta as *Jivan Mukti*, or Liberation in life, which is the goal of all Yogic movements, the very goal of life.

Lord Jesus taught in clear and concise terms that you must never forget the principal purpose of your existence: attainment of the Kingdom of Heaven, Liberation, *Nirvana*, Self-realization, release from the bondage of birth and death, cessation of sorrow.

> ***But rather seek ye the kingdom of God; and all these things shall be added unto you.***
> (KJV Luke 12: 31)

The quest for the highest goal implies integrating your personality, so that in this journey every part of your being becomes deeply involved and fulfilled. You seek God through your intellect by following the path of wisdom. You pursue Him through your heart by following the path of devotion. You seek to do His will by following the path of meditation and action. Human life must be a perpetual quest for the Kingdom of Heaven, for the attainment of God-realization.

Your Real Identity is Hidden

There is an interesting story about a tourist who went to Thailand to visit various Buddhist temples. In one temple he heard a remarkable story about the secret existence of a statue of Buddha made of solid gold. Some years before, Thailand was attacked by Burma. But before the Burmese invaded their country, the priests of the Thai temple pooled all their money, purchased gold, and sculpted it into the form of a Buddha. They then plastered the Buddha with multiple layers of mud so it appeared as though the statue was constructed of earth. During the war, all the Thai priests were killed and the great secret of the Buddha died along with the monks. The Buddha was left in the temple and remained cleverly disguised in mud for generations.

After some time, the priests that lived in the Thai temple decided to make some changes. They brought in a crane to relocate the Buddha. But as they were lifting the statue, the crane broke because the statue weighed more than a ton. The priests decided to leave the statue where it was since some cracks appeared as a result of it being dropped.

During the evening, when the head priest entered the shrine with a light to study the Buddha, he observed shimmering rays emanating from the Buddha's head. He thought he was surely witnessing the heavenly planes. But, upon closer observation, he realized that gold was peeking out from behind the layers of mud concealing the golden statue. So with great care, he gradually chiseled the mud away, and after some tedious effort, a brilliant Buddha emerged. He then understood the ingenious secret behind the mud.

This story offers you a symbolic lesson. Every human being is like the Golden Buddha, revealed when one patiently chisels away the mud that covers the true qualities of the soul. When the mud has been removed, one's Divine essence is revealed. You realize the hidden Truth that you have always been One with God, or in the words of Lord Jesus, "The Kingdom of Heaven is within Thee." You do not have to go anywhere to reach the state of Divine perfection.

Stop Searching through the Vast Realms of Illusion

Reflect on an interesting story, adapted from one written by Tolstoy that illustrates the vanity behind a life without purpose or spiritual value. A poor man traveled to a village looking for a job that would provide more material security. There he met a crafty, greedy and wealthy landowner who told him, "I will give you as much land as you want on one condition: At sunrise tomorrow you should start running and should not stop until sunset. Whatever land you circumscribe during that time shall be yours free of charge."

Unfortunately, the man was just as impoverished intellectually as he was financially. So he feverishly planned throughout the night how he would run in a vast circle to claim his land. He even worked out a mathematical formula that would ensure securing

Jesus preaching at the Sea of Galilee

the most land possible. When day broke, he began the race. On and on he went, running so much that by nightfall, just as he had completed encircling a vast tract of land, he had a heart attack, collapsed and died. The crafty landowner laughed and had the poor man's body put in a coffin and buried six feet under. That was the only land that he received.

Similar is the predicament of people who do not have a spiritual goal in life. If you do not seek the Kingdom of God within, if you do not have Liberation as your goal, then life is spent in trying to cover vast regions of this relative world-process, the realm of *maya* or illusion. And you go on doing so from incarnation to incarnation, trying to encircle as much "land" as possible from this world. But nothing is really tangible. As you exit from one embodiment and enter into another, you do not carry anything you acquired with you, for it is all left behind. Therefore, Lord Jesus says, *"But rather seek ye the kingdom of God; and all these things shall be added unto you."* (KJV Luke 12:31) Turn your mind to that great goal, the Kingdom of Heaven. Without it, all your attainments become vanities. With it, every attainment yields a purpose.

Seven Parables That Give Insight into the Kingdom of Heaven

Lord Jesus described the Kingdom of Heaven through parables. By gaining insight into these parables, one can understand that Jesus was not referring to a future time. He was asking people to bring about a change in their current state of consciousness so the Kingdom of Heaven could be realized at any moment.

Following are seven parables Lord Jesus told to give insight into the Kingdom of Heaven:

1. The Parable of the Sower

That same day Jesus left the house and went out beside Lake Galilee, where he sat down to teach. Such large crowds gathered around him that he had to sit in a boat, while the people stood on the shore. Then he taught them many things by using stories. He said, "A farmer went out to scatter seed in a field. While the farmer was scattering the seed, some of it fell along the road and was eaten by birds. Other seeds fell on thin, rocky ground and quickly started growing because the soil wasn't very deep. But when the sun came up, the plants were scorched and dried up, because they did not have enough roots. Some other seeds fell where thorny bushes grew up and choked the plants. But a few seeds did fall on good ground where the plants produced a hundred or sixty or thirty times as much as was scattered."
(CEV Matthew 13:1-8)

In the Parable of the Sower, when Jesus speaks about seeds that have been sown in various ways, He is speaking about the mind in various states of control. Mystically, the seeds are the teachings of the scriptures, and the farmer is the individual soul. The different states of mind are the fields where the seeds are sown.

In this parable one may see a close similarity to the Raja Yoga doctrine of the five states of the mind: dull, distracted, partially distracted, one-pointed, and controlled.

1. *Mudha:* A mind that is dull. Spiritual instructions do not become effective and are like seeds sown on the rocky ground, which germinate but soon wither and die.

2. *Kshipta:* A mind that is distracted. Teachings given to such a mind are wasted, like the seeds sown by the roadside that were eaten by birds before they could develop any roots.

3. *Vikshipta:* A partially distracted mind. Giving guidance to a person with this type of mind is like sowing seeds between thorny bushes; they grow, but are easily choked by lingering impressions of attachment, hatred, anger, greed and other thorny impediments. One who possesses a mind that is partially distracted needs to weed out the thorny mental impressions or *kleshas* (afflictions such as egoism, attachment and hatred) in order to advance on the spiritual path.

4. *Ekagrata:* A one-pointed mind. Such a mind is the fertile soil in which the teachings grow and flourish. This is the state of mind in an advanced

spiritual aspirant; the state that is conducive to lower *samadhi* (super-consciousness) and leads to the attainment of intuitive vision.

5. *Nirodha:* A controlled state of mind. This is the culminating or "harvesting" state of Yoga when the mind is absolutely immersed in the experience of the highest *samadhi*. During this state, the aspirant produces a "hundredfold" in the field, and thus experiences the expansion of his consciousness to infinity through God-realization.

2. The Parable of the Wheat and the Weeds

Jesus then told them this story:

"The Kingdom of Heaven is like what happened when a farmer scattered good seed in a field. But while everyone was sleeping, an enemy came and scattered weed seeds in the field and then left. When the plants came up and began to ripen, the farmer's servants could see the weeds. The servants came and asked, 'Sir, didn't you scatter good seed in your field? Where did these weeds come from?' 'An enemy did this,' he replied. His servants then asked, 'Do you want us to go out and pull up the weeds?' 'No!' he answered. 'You might also pull up the

wheat. Leave the weeds alone until harvest time. Then I'll tell my workers to gather the weeds and tie them up and burn them. But I'll have them store the wheat in my barn.'" (CEV Matthew 13:24-30)

This parable refers to the two types of unconscious impressions: pure and impure. Through spiritual practice, an aspirant reduces the impure impressions of attachment, hatred, and egoistic vision. In spite of his best efforts of exercising utmost vigilance in promoting pure impressions and eradicating those that are detrimental, certain negative impressions will continue to lurk in the unconscious. These, however, do not obstruct the rise of intuitive vision—"the wheat that is gathered in the barn." With intuitive vision, the impure impressions are spontaneously burned up in their entirety.

3. The Parable of the Mustard Seed

Jesus told them another story:

"The Kingdom of Heaven is like what happens when a farmer plants a mustard seed in a field. Although it is the smallest of all seeds, it grows larger than any garden plant and becomes a tree. Birds even come and nest on its branches." (CEV Matthew 13:31—32)

Like the subtle essence of the mustard seed that brings forth a tree, the subtle essence of one's heart (the Spirit) has the potential to unfold the entire universe within itself. In Chhandogya Upanishad, Shwetaketu is asked by his Guru, Sage Aruni, to break a tiny seed and see what lies within it. Shwetaketu replies that he sees nothing within the seed. Sage Aruni explains that in that subtle essence, which appears as nothing, a great tree is hidden. In the same way, human beings appear to be nothing and yet this whole universe, the subtle *Atman* or the Self, the innermost Reality, is hidden within every person.

4. The Parable of the Leaven

The kingdom of heaven is like what happens when a woman mixes a little yeast into three big batches of flour. Finally, all the dough rises. (CEV Matthew 13:33)

The Parable of the Leaven illustrates homogeneity in the Kingdom of Heaven. According to Vedanta philosophy, in the relative world of time and space one is trapped in an illusory triad. This triad (or "three measures of flour") can be thought of as "seer, seen and sight." "Seer" refers to you—the subject who experiences the world through the mind and senses. "Seen" refers to the world around you that you consider to be completely real. "Sight" refers to all your interacting experiences in that world. All three aspects of this triad are fraught with tremendous illusion due to the magic of *Maya* operating through the conditioned mind. This triad can also be equated with the three states of consciousness we experience every day in the form of waking, dream and deep sleep, as well as with the three "bodies" with which we are erroneously identified: physical, astral and causal.

When you add the "leaven" of Divine Love to each aspect of the triad, the illusory differences that constitute the world of relative reality disappear. When you attain Enlightenment or the Kingdom of Heaven, the three aspects of the triad merge in Pure Consciousness, much as leaven in bread becomes homogeneously blended. You understand that Pure Consciousness or the Divine Self alone exists. All else is *Maya*.

5. The Parable of the Hidden Treasure

> *The Kingdom of Heaven is like what happens when someone finds a treasure hidden in a field and buries it again. A person like that is happy and goes and sells everything in order to buy that field.*
> (CEV Matthew 13:44)

This parable illustrates the glory of spiritual abundance by allegorically describing the plot of an aspirant's life. Because of good karma from the past, you are able to sense that there is a treasure deep within your heart. Once that sensitivity develops, you focus wholeheartedly on retrieving that spiritual wealth.

Of course you pursue the project quietly. You do not advertise it. If you found a material treasure, you would keep your lips sealed until you got hold of it and had it completely under your control. Likewise, an aspirant should develop a similar spirit of inward secrecy. Your spiritual movement is a secret. How much you pray and meditate is a personal matter; it shouldn't be advertised for the sake of an outward show.

Once you are aware that the treasure exists, you sell everything you have—all your worldly values— to attain the field of pure mind that yields the Supreme Value of life. Through the practice of meditation and reflection, you dig deeply and joyously in that field until you attain the intuitive knowledge of the Self— the greatest of all treasures.

6. The Parable of the Pearl

The Kingdom of Heaven is like what happens when a shop owner is looking for fine pearls. After finding a very valuable

one, the owner goes and sells everything in order to buy that pearl.
(CEV Matthew 13:45-46)

This parable illustrates the attainment of perfect renunciation resulting in Self-realization. Having found the pearl of *Atman* (the Self), one negates the world of names and forms, considering them to be illusory.

7. The Parable of the Net

The Kingdom of Heaven is like what happens when a net is thrown into a lake and catches all kinds of fish. When the net is full, it is dragged to the shore, and the fishermen sit down to separate the fish. They keep the good ones, but throw the bad ones away.
(CEV Matthew 13:47-48)

Fishermen cast their net into the sea, gathering all types of fish—good and bad. Having hauled the net onto the beach, the fishermen select the fish that are good and toss away those that are bad. Similarly in life, one casts a net into the world and finds all types of circumstances, personalities and opportunities. Aspirants use their reflective mind to decipher what "fish" to keep for the purpose of reaching the Kingdom of Heaven and what "fish" to throw back into the ocean of the world.

Thus, in all these parables, Jesus does not ask you to wait to attain the Kingdom of Heaven, but rather to bring about a change and a transformation within to enter that Kingdom here and now. Similarly, in Yoga, the Kingdom of Heaven, also known as Self-realization or God-realization, is the intrinsic urge of life in every individual and is accomplished through the integration of reason, will, emotion, and action in day-to-day life. Reason is rendered into intuition, will is sublimated into the Divine Will, emotion is integrated into Divine Love, and action is permeated with a deeper sense of serving God at all times. Thus in the course of Yogic movement, every part of the personality is integrated and elevated until the Self is realized. In Self-realization, God is known to be the innermost Reality of all that exists. He is no longer seen as an entity existing outside of a person. Sages become one with God, eternally abiding in the Kingdom of Heaven while they continue treading the earth, sowing the seeds of Divine Bliss.

In the midst of the alternating experiences of pleasure and pain, remember that you are merely a traveler through the world-process. Always center your mind on the goal: The Kingdom of Heaven or God-realization. With joy in your heart, gain the insight that intrinsically you are one with God, that you have been fashioned in the "Image of God." The beautiful teaching of Lord Jesus, *"The Kingdom of Heaven is within thee,"* is also expressed in the Upanishadic statement, *"Tat Twam Asi"*— "Thou Art That."

Alluding to the state of Liberation (the attainment of the Kingdom of Heaven), St. John says in Revelations:

> **And there shall be no night there; and they need no candle, neither light of the sun; for Lord God gives them light; and they shall reign forever and ever.**
> (KJV Revelations 22:5)

A similar statement is given in Kathopanishad, describing the state of Liberation:

> **There the sun does not shine; the moon, stars, lightning and fire—none of these have access to that realm. It is by the light of the Self that all these shine.**

These statements from the Christian and Vedantic scriptures reveal that one who has attained the Kingdom of Heaven has acquired the mystic knowledge that is the radiance in the sun, the illumination of the moon, the surging of the ocean and the dynamism of the wind—that which is the Beauty of the beautiful, the Joy of the joyous, the Essence of all—one's very Self.

Chapter Nine

Discover Your Spiritual Treasure

In the Sermon on the Mount, Lord Jesus says:

> *Lay not up for yourselves treasures upon earth, where moth and rust doth corrupt, and where thieves break through and steal: But lay up for yourselves treasures in Heaven, where neither moth nor rust doth corrupt, and where thieves do not break through nor steal: For where your treasure is, there will your heart be also.*
> (KJV Matthew 6:19-21)

A statement in the Upanishads provides a definition of the treasure that everyone is seeking:

> *The Divine treasure is an effulgent treasure and that effulgent treasure lies within your heart.*

Lord Jesus reflects the Upanishadic wisdom by saying, "*The Kingdom of Heaven is within thee.*" In order to discover the Divine Treasure, one must look to the imperishable and eternal Divine basis within one's own heart.

In contrast, the treasures on earth as well as all earthly achievements are perishable. This includes your body, possessions, relatives, and circumstances, which are all subject to change. If your mind constantly invests its energy in things that are not abiding, such as your physical appearance, fashions, clothes, and other vanities, in spite of your external riches you will remain internally poor and miserable.

In the light of Eastern philosophy, you are a soul moving from embodiment to embodiment. In each embodiment you created an earthly treasure in the form of possessions, the objects to which you were attached. But then, by the inscrutable process of time, you moved from one embodiment and entered into another. What happened to all your treasures? Most people invest their energy in accumulating and multiplying wealth. But very few people give attention to how to utilize their wealth. Wealth you have accumulated and earned in your lifetime should be utilized for your deeper fulfillment. The purpose of wealth is not to provide mere enjoyments of the senses, but to help you perform good deeds that promote a sublime relationship to God within yourself.

When wealth is a means to spiritual advancement, that wealth is blessed. But when wealth becomes only a means to pamper the ego and promote an uncontrolled and undisciplined mind, then that wealth becomes a curse. If you lack true satisfaction, peace, and serenity within your heart, the wealth and power you possess is meaningless, even when you have attained all that you want externally in this world.

Life should be lived in such a way that your mind recognizes the greatest treasure: the attainment of Self-realization, the awareness that you and God are one, the direct knowledge that the Kingdom of Heaven is within you. If you are truly rich, there will be an overwhelming sense of tranquility and harmony within your personality.

When you have earthly treasures, you can never relax. The greater the treasure, the greater is your worry and anxiety. Spiritual treasure is devoid of all those worries. This higher definition of treasure does not imply that you should not have material conveniences, but material things should be a means to an end and should not outweigh your spiritual aspiration.

An episode from the life of Alexander the Great illustrates his awareness of the impermanence of material wealth. Although his life was short, before his death he had conquered most of the civilized world as well as affluent countries, thereby accumulating immense wealth. But before dying, his instructions were that after his death his hands should be outstretched so that people understood that he carried nothing with him.

Jesus Is Tested by Satan

There is an important point that is well illustrated in the temptations that were presented by Satan to Jesus after His forty days of austerity and fasting. Satan asked Jesus to use His power to convert stones into bread to satisfy His hunger. But Jesus asserted, *"Man shall not live by bread alone, but by every word that proceedeth out of the mouth of God."* (KJV Matthew 4:7)Then Satan asked Him to jump off a high pinnacle to show the world how He is sustained by the angels. But Jesus scolded Satan and did not submit to his request, saying, *"It is written again, Thou shalt not tempt the Lord thy God."* (KJV Matthew 4:7) Finally, Satan displayed all the treasures of the world and promised to give them all to Jesus, if only He would bow down to Satan. But Jesus would not do so, responding, *"Away from me, Satan! For it is written: Worship the Lord your God, and serve Him only."* (NIV Matthew 4: 10)

This story gives insight into the fact that one who wishes to enter the Kingdom of Heaven (attain Self-realization) is not tempted by material attainments, psychic powers, and all the glories of the world. One may attain all of these, and yet there is no real inner fulfillment. They are all fake treasures because one's

heart continues to yearn for God. What, then, is the use of bowing to Satan for worldly attainments if one's heart is unfulfilled? Why shouldn't one bow to God and attain infinite Bliss?

Shat Sampat—The Six-fold Treasure of Virtues

The Vedantic texts describe a six-fold treasure known as *Shat Sampat*. The foremost quality to attain is serenity of the mind—*shama*. *Shama* cannot be developed if you believe that certain happenings are going to give you perpetual satisfaction. If one depends upon the world for happiness, the mind will always be agitated. Real happiness does not depend upon external happenings. Instead it depends upon maintaining the Kingdom of Heaven as one's main focus while enjoying a calm and relaxed mind. Instead of allowing your mind to become scattered or agitated, live life with great precision, dynamism, enthusiasm and persistence. There lies the secret of all religions. The ocean in its depth is calm, although on the surface there is a constant activity of countless waves. Real happiness abides deep within your heart.

To maintain serenity, observe your mind in the same way that a person who is interested in worldly wealth focuses on every penny day by day so that his business does not suffer a loss. By fighting and quarreling over trivial matters, people become great losers in spiritual wealth and waste their mental energy. Lack of patience, understanding, adaptability and endurance cause agitation in the human mind. When you lose your mental balance over little things, you are throwing away your spiritual treasure.

The next treasure among the six-fold virtues is *dama*, the control of senses. The world cannot be experienced without the senses, which are a wondrous gift of God allowing you to admire the Divine creation. As Lord Jesus says, *"Behold the lilies of the field, how do they grow?"* The senses should generate an awareness of Divine majesty, instead of restlessness and mental craving that thrive when the senses dominate the mind. When the senses operate under the guidance of reason, they bring to you a feeling of Divine Presence. The world becomes a vast temple where the birds are singing the glory of God, the breeze whispers of eternity, and the sun pours down its effulgence as if it is declaring the luminosity of God.

From a practical point of view, the art of *dama* implies living a life of rhythmic balance, not extremes. There is a time to sleep, a time to wake up, a time for activity, according to your circumstances. But life should not be lived abruptly. If your life is not balanced, the senses become your master. If your life is harmonious, the senses become servants of the advancing mind.

Uparati, the third virtue, implies detaching from the fruits of selfish actions, performing your responsibilities for purity of heart rather than external achievement. You learn to renounce what pertains to the little self and welcome what pertains to the Supreme Self.

Through the fourth virtuous quality, *titiksha* or endurance, one learns how to endure difficult physical and psychological situations. Train your body to endure the little variations of weather so that your energy is not spent trying to create more desirable conditions. A worldly person may completely rearrange the things in their room so that every flower or object is precisely placed according to their taste, and each window is opened to a certain angle to let in a particular type of breeze. However, by the time every detail is settled and they finally prepare to relax, a cockroach may enter the room, disturbing the peace of the person who worked so hard to create external perfection. Without endurance, a sense of frustration depletes the energy of the mind.

Mental endurance is also necessary to face situations in which you are not understood, even by your closest friends and relatives. Lacking *titiksha*, long-time friends may dissolve their friendship for the smallest of reasons. When there is *titiksha*, you wait with patience without the ego demanding fulfillment of its expectations.

The next virtuous treasure is *shraddha*, faith in God. Faith is not a sentimental development, but has to be cultivated with great perseverance. If a religious person gives a sermon that causes you to proclaim, "Now I have faith," your faith is probably not real. Rather, abiding faith develops gradually like a tree. By performing good deeds, attending *satsanga* or good association, and living a righteous life, you will witness its growth. When these are blended together, your faith deepens. You will realize that the world is a product of God's infinite wisdom, and you are placed in every situation that is best suited for your advancement.

Indeed, always work to better your situation, because God has also planted within your mind the possibility of improving your circumstances to make them more fulfilling. But avoid an attitude of either despair or craving; rather, maintain a sense of deep satisfaction and tranquility. You are living in a world that is created by a God Who is omniscient and omnipotent. Therefore, there isn't any obstacle that you cannot conquer with Divine assistance. From the point of view of ego, you can do very little. But with God dwelling within your heart, nothing is impossible.

The last treasure is *samadhana*, the tranquil flow of mind to God. *Samadhana* enables the mind to remain balanced without developing contradiction with varying situations. If it's cold and raining, rejoice instead of frowning about the humidity, the temperature, or the cold draft. Understand that conditions are exactly what you wanted—not you as the ego, but You as God. And since it is God's will that delights you more than your ego, there will be a sense of relaxation and serenity.

If these six-fold virtues are developed, they are the treasures that point to the Ultimate Treasure: The Kingdom of Heaven, or the attainment of God-realization. *"Where your treasure lies,"* says Lord Jesus, *"there is your heart."* If God becomes your treasure, your heart will be in God. Your eyes will become single, and you will be nothing but Light. Great will be that Light, the Light that goes beyond the light of the sun, moon, and stars. It is the Light of Wisdom.

Can a Wealthy Man Enter into the Kingdom of Heaven?

And again I say unto you, it is easier for a camel to go through the eye of a needle, than for a rich man to enter into the Kingdom of God. (KJV Matthew 19:24)

That reference to "camel" did not literally mean the familiar desert animal; what it really referred to were the large ropes that were used on ancient boats. As time passed, the true meaning faded away. It really doesn't matter, however, whether the term refers to the rope or the animal, because neither could ever pass through the eye of a needle! In the same way, a selfish and greedy person who is proud of his attachment to material attainment could never enjoy the Kingdom of God.

So the statement of Lord Jesus is literally true to a very great extent. People who are burdened with the pride of wealth cannot advance spiritually. However, there are many wealthy people who do not have this prideful sense of possession, and there are many poor people who are thoroughly attached to the few things that they have. It is this inward attachment, rather than the external circumstance, that obstructs spiritual realization.

You may think that since the ascetics and *sanyasins* living in Himalayan caves have no wealth, the Kingdom of Heaven will immediately open up for them. But this is not necessarily so, because unenlightened ascetics can be terribly attached to and dependent upon the few things that they do have. They may have only a broken cup, but if you were to take it away from them, they would become furious with rage.

Attachment is like a piece of leather. Leather expands in heat and contracts in cold. Whether it is in a contracted or expanded state, the leather is still there. In the same way, wealthy people can be attached to many things, so attachment becomes expanded. On the other hand, poor people can be attached to only a few things, and in this case, attachment has become contracted. However, it is the very same attachment that will not allow the person to progress on the spiritual path. As long as you are attached to the objects of the world, as long as you are proud of possessing things, and as long as you are internally caught up in entanglements, you cannot enter the Kingdom of Heaven.

External or material prosperity is not healthy unless it is accompanied by internal prosperity. Unless your material success is accompanied by the development of Divine qualities within your personality, it is not healthy prosperity. People can become externally rich without having any inner wealth at all. If so, they are certainly not prosperous in any real sense.

If you burden a donkey with sandalwood, the donkey doesn't enjoy the sandalwood. It simply becomes a burden. Similarly, if a greedy person acquires an abundance of wealth and he does not have sublime intentions for that fortune, that abundance is the same as a burden of sandalwood on a donkey's back. What many wealthy people feel during their lifetime is the intense pressure from their wealth— the burden. After carrying that burden, they depart, leaving the load for somebody else to carry. Can that be called prosperity?

Chapter Ten

Drink from the Well of Divine Love and Wisdom

The Biblical episodes described in John 4:1-34, summarized below, give you a glimpse of the wondrous teachings and the majestic personality of Jesus:

Jesus had started His ministry and was performing miracles, healing the sick, and traveling through the dusty roads of Samaria. As He wandered with His handful of disciples, He became very tired and thirsty. His disciples went to the market for food. Left alone and thirsty, Jesus sat by Jacob's Well, a reservoir built in ancient times. While He rested there, a Samarian lady approached the well and started drawing water. Although the Jewish people of that time considered Samarians to be outcasts, Jesus asked this Samarian woman for some water to quench His thirst.

Seeing Jesus as a personality to be revered, she said, "Don't you know from whom You are

asking water? I am a Samarian lady and I should not give you water." Jesus replied, "If you knew with Whom you are speaking, you wouldn't say that. I am the Giver of Eternal Water—the Water that gives immortality." She said, "You have no ropes, no vessel to draw water out of the well, yet you say you are going to give the Water of Life." Jesus explained, "With the water you drink from this well, you become thirsty again and again, but the well of Eternal Water surges with Water that satisfies all your thirst forever with fulfillment and joy." She became attentive and said wearily, "I am tired of coming to this well again and again to draw water. I would like to have your Water and you can have mine." She gave him water to drink and they talked about philosophical matters.

This episode has a profound spiritual meaning. Although the Bible does not mention this, the implication is very clear. The Samarian lady is a symbol of the individual soul, a *jiva* who comes into the world-process. The well refers to the source of pleasure through the senses, which is the water that people run after in this world. You go after those waters, the perishable pleasures of the senses, and again become thirsty. Day by day you must draw water, coming back again and again. This implies being born again and again—the repeated cycles of birth and death. The *jiva* visiting the well goes on drawing water that does not quench its thirst but, rather, increases it.

However, there comes a time when an individual soul attains a state of purity through positive karmas of the past and encounters Divine inspiration, a Divine Contact. This is symbolized by the Samarian lady, who with purity of heart and humility encounters Jesus. Then, the soul glimpses that immortalizing Water, the Water of Divine Love, of Divine Wisdom, the "Water" that the soul is thirsting for embodiment after embodiment.

In order to acquire that Water of Divine Love that abides in the depths of the human heart, let the water you are now experiencing in your life, the water of sense pleasure, be dedicated to Lord Jesus. Let Jesus, Who is within your heart, enjoy all your delights. Offer what little you have and Jesus will manifest in the form of Divine Consciousness to give the Spiritual Water that leads to Immortality.

In the same chapter, when the Samarian lady said, "Oh Jesus, I am interested in your water," Jesus replied, "Come have a drink of that Water and bring your husband as well." She said, "I have no husband." Then Jesus told her, "Well said. You have had five husbands and the man with you now is not your husband. Therefore, what you say is true." And she said, "How do You know this? Surely, You are the Messiah."

The story is packed with symbolism. In Indian tradition, it is easy to understand that five husbands refer to the five subtle and gross elements (earth, water, fire, air and ether) that compose the world, and the man that Jesus referred to as not her husband denotes the ego. *Jiva* has been wedded to the five elements and the ego, but when purity develops, the soul discards the world of elements. It develops dispassion and gains an insight into the futility of the ego. It is then that Jesus invites the soul into the depths of the heart, where the soul drinks the Water from the mystic well.

Continuing the enlightening teachings of this chapter, the lady asked Jesus where a person should perform worship. Jesus explained that although people go to worship in different places, a time is coming when they will not be worshipping in places, but within their own hearts and in spirit. In the spirit lies the genuine place where one should offer worship. The implication again is very simple: Divine worship is not confined to physical locations of worship or to external rituals; it expresses in a changed state of personality, a changed attitude within one's heart. Whatever you do should become a form of worship. Indeed, life itself can become a perpetual process of worship.

While the conversation continued, the disciples returned, bringing food from the market. They were surprised that He, who was supposed to be very tired and thirsty, was holding a pleasant conversation instead of lying down and waiting for sustenance. So when Jesus knew what the disciples were thinking, He turned to them and said, "The food that sustains me is different from the provisions that you have brought. The food that sustains Me comes from God. The Divine Will I perform is my nourishment, and it is that which sustains me. That "food" does not depend upon a future harvest time. That eternal harvest is right now; the harvest is ready and the corn is ripe."

Christ, speaking in riddles said,

"Some plant the seed, and others harvest the crop. I am sending you to harvest crops in fields where others have done all the hard work." (CEV John 4:37-38)

The implication is that Sages and Saints have sown seeds and have established a spiritual basis. Those who develop purity of heart enter a mystical field to reap the harvest. What is the harvest that Jesus refers to? It is the harvest of spiritual joy and fulfillment. Good thoughts, charitable acts, generosity, humility and faith are like seeds of everlasting values sown deep within one's heart. When the harvest manifests, it is a harvest of Eternal Life.

To help you to better understand Christ's simile of spiritual Bliss versus the fruit of a normal harvest,

Buddha

there is a parable from the Buddhist tradition that
illustrates this point:

A farmer had cultivated his land, reaped his
harvest, and stored the produce in large sacks inside

his barn. One cold, wintery night, dark clouds gathered and torrential rains descended. The farmer, seated by the fireside, was joyous and content, knowing that he had performed his duty. He had collected the harvest and was inside his house with his wife and family. He thought to himself, "Who could be more deserving and prosperous than I am?"

Suddenly lightning flashed and through the window he saw Buddha seated under a tree for protection. The farmer mistakenly thought he was a simple vagrant. Seeing him, the farmer called out to him with ridicule, saying, "Here is a man who has escaped his duties, and has not done his work in the fields." He then sang, "Oh rain, come! Oh clouds, bring torrents abundant with thunder and lightning! What have I to be afraid of? I have collected my grains; I am filled with satisfaction."

When Buddha heard the farmer mocking him, he also laughed and sang, "Oh torrential rain, come! I too have gathered my produce from the field. But my field is abundant with the seeds of love, understanding, non-violence, goodness, and contentment. I have watered those seeds and looked after my field with constant meditation. My harvest is *Nirvana* (Liberation). I have unending attainment, so why should I be afraid of rain and clouds?"

When the farmer realized that this was a Divine personality, his thinking suddenly changed. He came out of his house and kneeled at the feet of Buddha. In time, he became Buddha's follower.

Jesus spoke about that harvest that doesn't require tilling the soil or sowing the seeds. Sages and Saints have taught the art of mystical farming from ancient times. In the fertile soil of your purified heart, you sow the seeds of humility, devotion and other Divine virtues. You will then reap the harvest of Nirvana, the Kingdom of Heaven, Liberation.

Chapter Eleven

Ascend the Heights of Detachment

As described in the New Testament, Lord Jesus gave a profound message to his closest disciples:

...I have not come to bring peace, but a sword. For I have come to turn man against his father, a daughter against her mother, a daughter-in-law against her mother-in-law.
(NIV Matthew 10: 34-35)

This is a shocking statement. Everyone knows that Jesus came to establish peace. But then, what did He mean by this paradoxical statement? And what was He expressing when He continued:

He that loveth father or mother more than Me is not worthy of Me: and he that loveth son or daughter more than Me is not worthy of Me. And he that taketh not his Cross, and followeth after Me, is not worthy of me. He that findeth his life shall lose it: and he that

loseth his life for My sake shall find it.
(KJV Matthew 10: 37—39)

When Jesus states that He had come with a sword to turn man against his father, a daughter against her mother, a daughter-in-law against her mother–in-law, He is referring to doing battle with the attachments and illusions that are based on egoism. The relatives represent the deluded attitudes one holds towards worldly relationships: "He is mine, she is mine, these children are mine." These attitudes are fundamentally based on fear. The more you intensify the feelings of attachment—the I-ness and mine-ness known in Sanskrit as *ahamta* and *mamata*—the more you intensify the cloud of ignorance that blocks out the luminous Light of God. Just as clouds shut out the shining sun, so do these illusions of ownership. They form the fabric of the world-process and drive one to constantly wander from one birth to the next in the vain pursuit of achievements that ultimately end in emptiness.

However, when you turn to God, He descends upon you with a sword of Light. As the sun rises, it sends forth swords of light that pierce the heart of darkness. From the point of view of the darkness, the sun is a terrible force that comes to destroy it with a sword, turning relative against relative. But from the point of view of the light, it is a wondrous development. Similarly, God within the heart tears asunder the illusions created by the mind steeped in the darkness of ignorance, the very cause of pain and suffering. When this happens, there unfolds the unimaginable beauty of Divine Love, the ultimate source of peace and supreme joy.

In another statement Lord Jesus says:

And everyone that hath forsaken houses or brethren or sisters or father or mother or wife or children or lands for my name's sake shall receive a hundred-fold, and shall inherit everlasting life.
(KJV Matthew 19:29)

If you follow this literally you will conclude that if you renounce one husband, you'll acquire one hundred husbands in Heaven, or if you renounce your mother, you will have a hundred mothers in Heaven. But of course, you cannot interpret these teachings literally. This is why mystical teachings need to be understood under guidance.

This statement is not meant to create a sense of disharmony. What it really implies is that God should be loved in all relations. It is from the ego's standpoint that someone is your father, mother or child. From a higher standpoint, you recognize that God alone is in all. When you understand that God is embodied in all human beings, you are sacrificing the ego's value. You are sacrificing your father when you realize that the Divine Self is within him and you serve God in him. You are sacrificing your mother when you begin to serve her, not as a mother, but as God in the form of mother.

Advanced religion implies developing a penetrating attitude by turning away from the limited names and forms and embracing what is truly behind those names and forms. Religion becomes profound when your dealings with others are not based on ego, but rather are based on the understanding that God is the Indweller in all.

Develop the understanding that God is within everyone. When you do this, you sacrifice your ego's values and gain a hundredfold in return. The egoistic love that you experienced in lesser manifestations was fleeting and insignificant. It was shrouded in illusion. But when you begin to love God in all names and forms, you experience the profundity of Divine Love. Then you have gained a thousand fathers, a thousand mothers, and everything you wanted.

This state is like *chintamani* (the wish-yielding jewel). In Hindu mysticism it refers to a rare jewel that fulfills all your desires, but not in an ordinary way. They are fulfilled beyond your expectations.

The ideal behind every religion is to discover the love of God. Just as a fish out of water struggles to return to the water, so too, every soul yearns to love God and be reunited with Him. Unfortunately, this yearning is obstructed by numerous illusions: "This is me. These are mine. I have done all this work to secure my happiness and that of my family. How great am I!" Illusions such as these prevent a person from communing with God and reaching the ultimate state of fulfillment. This is why Lord Jesus said, *"He that loveth father or mother more than me is not worthy of me...."*

Develop the great insight that all living beings are sustained by God. It is God Who shines through the eyes of the child that a mother holds in her arms. It is God Who operates through your beloved, your friends and dearest relatives. When you develop this insight, you adore God while serving your relatives.

The ideal that one must love God in others is one of the foundations of the Hindu religion. Saint Kabira sang: *"Ghat ghat me hai sain ramata katuka vachan mat bol re"*—"In every individual abides the Lord; therefore, do not speak harsh words." Rather, seize every opportunity that God gives you to serve others. Be careful not to create egoistic impressions of *dwesha* (hatred) as well as impressions of *raga* (attachment). These illusions abide on the two sides of the same coin. One is an indication of the other's existence.

In general, people are confused about the meaning of "detachment" because this is a very subtle and advanced philosophical concept. If you do not understand the concept properly, you may misinterpret it to mean that you should be cold, indifferent, or even cruel. A person who has just attended a Yoga lecture about *vairagya* or detachment might go back home and tell his relatives, "I'm no longer attached to you. Do whatever you want. Let the baby cry! I don't care. I'm detached!" But that is not the real meaning of detachment.

Detachment is meant to withdraw you from your illusions and direct your vision to the Divine within each person. To the extent you withdraw from illusory forms of love and attachment, to that extent a more profound love unfolds within your heart towards others. A love of this sort is like sunlight. When the sun rises, clouds catch the rays and begin to glow, decked with multicolored attire. Similarly, as more profound love unfolds in your heart, it touches every aspect of your personality, endowing it with luminosity and magnanimity.

There is a parable that vividly illustrates the imprisoning nature of attachment. There was once a king who was especially fond of his pet hawk. It was his custom to take the hawk to a nearby forest to hunt with him. Often, while flying over the forest, the hawk would pass over a hut where an old woman lived, and he would fly down and peer inside. It seemed like such a congenial and cozy place to the hawk, and there was usually a warm fire glowing in the fireplace. Whenever the woman saw the bird, she would beckon him, saying, "Come little child. Come take some delicious food by the fire."

On one occasion, the hawk decided to enter the old woman's hut, thinking that it would be wonderful to live in a warm place with someone who would give him so much love. No sooner had he flown through the window than the woman caught hold of him, tied a string around his neck, and clipped some of his feathers so he could not fly. As she did so, she said, "I'm doing all this just for you because I love you. Stay here with me forever." And so the hawk became a prisoner. From the woman's point of view it was out of love, and the hawk became enticed. But the moment he did so, he lost his freedom of flight.

Love based on attachment runs the same course. When you love someone with attachment, your ego is always planning to tie that person down so that he or she may always stay as close to you as possible. When your love is conditioned by attachment, you have unwittingly created bondage, not only for the other person, but for yourself as well. When higher love develops, however, you realize the joy of inner freedom for yourself as well as for the other person. You no longer feel threatened by the possibility that the person may leave you. Your purpose then becomes one of helping the soul, rather than tying it down. Unless there is deeper love, one cannot let go of lesser love. As you discover the deeper love of God, attachments melt away, and you find that you have no expectations as you perform duties for the people you love. The very fact that you have loved another person and helped that person grow is fulfilling.

A simple illustration is a mother's love for her child. The mother's love for the child is so exhilarating that she expects nothing in return. Have you ever heard of a mother who itemized all the expenses for her child's care and then presented the bill to him when he had grown up? The fact is that the child's very presence is deeply rewarding to her.

When you have spiritual love in your heart, you do not develop attachments, because the joy you feel surpasses ordinary human love. This is the implication of Christ's statement: "*He that loveth father or mother more than me is not worthy of me.*" The moment your mind becomes caught up by names and forms like "mother" and "father," you develop attachment; you want to tie down different individuals in the network of *raga*. But when you develop Divine Love, you are spontaneously sacrificing, self-effacing, enduring and forgiving, just as a mother is with her child. Thus a love that waits, sacrifices, and inspires emanates from your heart when attachments fade.

The message of Christ, and indeed of every religion, is to transcend your ego, dissolve its illusions, and live to recognize the Divine Self in all. If you do so, there will then be the most profound fulfillment within your heart, and you will discover a treasure that never perishes. You will become truly wealthy in the spiritual sense.

Chapter Twelve
Be Born in the Spirit

The secret of spiritual life lies in being born in the Spirit. Satan represents the ego. When you are born in the body, you identify with your ego. You belong to a particular family, race, religion, country or financial status and the ego is very proud of all these. Ego gives you the feeling of either being superior or inferior to others because of the values determined by society. In this way, you are identified with a limited personality who is subject to birth and death. Your attainments are confined to this world of time and space. Your life is as short as a dewdrop hanging from a leaf, trembling at every puff of breeze that blows.

Your ego is proud of your attainments—a family, a home, education, a career, fame, financial status, spiritual authority in a church, etc. And although you must be practical in pursuing these things, keep in mind that a strong dependence on them implies that you have built your "house" on the shifting sands of illusion. The rains of affliction beat upon the roof of that house, and the storms of adversities shake its very foundation. In other words, these things are not necessarily permanent throughout your lifetime. To continue to depend on them at the risk of losing your mental balance implies that you continue to exist in a state of bondage, of karmic involvement, of repeated cycles of birth and death. This is the point that is illustrated by Lord Jesus:

> *Therefore whoever hears these sayings of Mine, and does them, I will liken him to a wise man who built his house on the rock: and the rain descended, the floods came, and the winds blew and beat on that house; and it did not fall, for it was founded on the rock. But everyone who hears these sayings of Mine, and does not do them, will be like a foolish man who built his house on the sand: and the rain descended, the floods came, and the winds blew and beat on that house; and it fell. And great was its fall.*
> (KJV Matthew 7:24-26)

When you are born in Spirit, you continue to maintain your practical realities to the very best of your ability. However, inwardly you feel that you no longer belong to a particular family, race, financial status, church, country, or to a world defined by time and space. From a worldly perspective, you may be very successful or wealthy. However, you gradually learn to release the strong mental and emotional dependency on worldly acquisitions and begin to identify with God Who dwells within. You belong to the Spirit, which is universal, non-dual, eternal, unborn, infinite and dwells within all that exists. You belong to the Universal family and honor all beings and all things. You no longer tremble during storms of insecurity that sweep over all objects and attainments of this world. You have built your house on the solid rock that Jesus speaks about, and you are not shaken even during the torrential rains of afflictions and the raging winds of adversities. Freed from the cycles of birth and death, you enjoy unbounded bliss and limitless peace! You have attained the Kingdom of Heaven of the Bible, the *Nirvana* of the Buddhists, the *Moksha* of Vedanta—the highest goal of all mystical movements.

What Is Spiritual Rebirth?

Now there was a Pharisee, a man named Nicodemus who was a member of the Jewish ruling council. He came to Jesus at night and said, "Rabbi, we know that You are a teacher Who has come from God. For no one could perform the signs You are doing if God were not with Him." Jesus

replied, "Very truly I tell you, no one can see the Kingdom of God unless they are born again." "How can someone be born when they are old?" Nicodemus asked. "Surely they cannot enter a second time into their mother's womb to be born!" Jesus answered, "Very truly I tell you, no one can enter the Kingdom of God unless they are born of water and the Spirit."
(NIV John 3:1-5)

In this story in the New Testament, Nicodemus was bewildered by what Jesus meant by rebirth. This puzzle must also be resolved by aspirants. The art of spiritual rebirth sprouts in the form of aspiration, matures into the tree of spiritual discipline, unfolds the blossoms of Divine virtues, and bears the fruit of immortality. Only when one is born of Water (Divine Love) and of the Spirit (Wisdom) is one truly born in Spirit. When *bhakti* (devotion) and *jnana* (wisdom) blend within the personality, the aspirant ascends to the majestic heights of spiritual consciousness.

You must be twice-born to enter the Kingdom of God. Normal human birth confines you to the family of mortals. However, with the vision of your deeper Self, spiritual birth dawns within your personality. Thus born, you relate yourself to the family of Sages and Saints, and to the world of the immortals.

"How can a man be born when he is old?" asked Nicodemus. Jesus explained to him that spiritual birth is not a physical event that can be seen by one's eyes. All spiritual unfoldment is beyond the range of the senses. Jesus states,

> *The Spirit is like the wind that blows wherever it wants to. You can hear the wind, but you don't know where it comes from or where it is going.*
> (CEV John 3:8)

With spiritual rebirth, one resembles the wind that does not come from a particular place, or go to a particular place, yet the sound is heard and the effect is seen. The lives of enlightened Sages are not confined, and their bountiful effects are seen in their Divine works. Wind infuses life and vitality into living beings. Sages who have entered the Kingdom of Heaven (Enlightenment) have attained spiritual rebirth and continue to infuse harmony, peace, and upliftment in humanity.

Similar was the explanation presented by Buddha when a disciple asked him where a man goes in the state of Liberation. He blew out a candle and asked the disciple where the flame had gone. The passage of the flame cannot be seen. So too, the movement of the Spirit cannot be interpreted in the language of the senses.

Which Path Will You Choose:
The Pleasant or the Blessed?

Enter through the narrow gate. For wide is the gate and broad is the road that leads to destruction, and many enter through it. But small is the gate and narrow the road that leads to life, and only a few find it.
(KJV Matthew 7:13-14)

Lord Jesus encourages his disciples to tread the blessed path that leads to the Kingdom of Heaven. Even though that path is difficult, it frees an aspirant from the trap of the world-process and its repeated cycles of birth and death.

The Upanishads speak of two paths: The path of *preya* (that which is pleasant) and the path of *shreya* (that which is blessed). The former is the movement of externalization, characterized by increasing dependence on the senses and worldly objects. The latter is the internalized movement characterized by growing detachment towards the objects of the world, and increasing attachment to God or the Divine Self. When you adopt the path of *shreya* (the path of blessedness), you enter the narrow gate. Though the path seems difficult in the beginning, it becomes increasingly delightful as you experience inner peace and fulfillment. Do not live for the ego-self, represented by Satan in the Bible, but live to discover the fact that you are the

Universal Self underlying the ego-self. This demands constant negation of the ego and affirmation of the Universality of the Self.

Selfless service of humanity, prayer, reflection, devout meditation on God, development of Divine qualities, cultivation of Divine Love and Wisdom— these are the methods that must be pursued in your daily life in order to "die" to the ego-self and be reborn in the Spirit. As you enter into higher spiritual realms through devotion, you gradually and spontaneously develop dispassion towards all that is attainable in the realms of the not-Self (the senses, mind and intellect). You integrate your personality so well that the confines of the body and mind are surpassed, and you enter into the transcendental Kingdom of Heaven. The strings of your personality are so wonderfully tuned that they bring forth the melody of eternity.

Born in the realm of ignorance, you have a beginning and an end. You move in the world of time and space. But when you are born of the Spirit, you discover your innate spiritual nature. You are no longer identified with your body. You rise above ego-consciousness and discover your unity with the Divine Self.

Chapter Thirteen

You Are the Light of the World

Ye are the light of the world. A city that is set on a hill cannot be hid. Neither do men light a candle, and put it under a bushel, but on a candlestick; and it giveth light unto all that are in the house. Let your light so shine before men, that they may see your good works, and glorify your Father which is in Heaven. (KJV Matthew 5:14-16)

The simile of Light is a predominant feature in Upanishadic literature, the literature of the Vedas. *"Jyotisham api tad jyotih"*—"You are the Light of lights." Light is that which illuminates. Your senses have an important role in illuminating the world. If you did not have the senses, you would not be able to perceive the world. It is only through the senses that you become aware of a world where you can see, hear, touch, taste, and smell.

But then, the senses by themselves cannot illumine things. What illuminates the senses is the mind. What illuminates the mind is the intellect. What illuminates the intellect is the Divine Self. That Divine Self is your essential identity. You are not the ego-personality. You are the Light of lights. If you were to discover that Divine identity and become enlightened through a process of spiritual discipline, devotion, meditation, wisdom, and righteous action, you would become *"a city that is set on a hill—a city that cannot be hidden."*

Neither do men light a candle, and put it under a bushel, but on a candlestick; and it giveth light unto all that are in the house.

When you are in a dark house, the moment you turn on a lamp that has been placed in a suitable location, the entire house is lit up. Similarly, when your main focus is Enlightenment, you are placing your light in a favorable location. You are essentially the Light of lights, but that Light must be used effectively to enlighten the mind. Attainment of Enlightenment has two aspects: subjective and objective. Subjectively, you become free of all mental pain and sorrow. Objectively, you become a Guiding Light to the world around you. The Light of God shines through the mind of an enlightened Sage or Saint, and from that enlightened mind other people receive inspiration and guidance. As time passes, that Light of spiritual illumination continues to touch the lives of many. If, however, you do not follow the path of Enlightenment, you have put that potential Light that dwells within you under a bushel and it will provide neither you nor the people around you with illumination.

> *Let your light so shine before men, that they may see your good works, and glorify your Father which is in Heaven.*

You are allowing *"your light so shine before men"* when goodness expresses through your personality, when a situation provokes your mind to anger or revenge and you do not retaliate. Worship of God from a more profound level implies creating a tremendous transformation within your own personality, so that your heart becomes a temple. Your thoughts, your feelings, your words and your actions become fundamental ingredients for worshipping God. They all waft the aroma of Divine worship. You express the glory of God through the very life that you live.

Chapter Fourteen

You Are the Salt of the Earth

You are the salt of the earth, but if salt has lost its taste, how shall its saltiness be restored? It is no longer good for anything except to be thrown out and trampled under people's feet. (KJV Matthew 5:13)

If wonderful dishes of food are prepared, but salt is not present, you cannot enjoy the variations of taste. In saying this, we are not speaking from a culinary or even medical point of view, but from a symbolic and spiritual viewpoint. Generally, salt adds relish to every type of food you eat. Similarly, life and all its experiences should contain a special relish. If you know how to put a little sprinkle of "salt" in everything you experience—pain as well as pleasure—life becomes easier.

To most people, pleasant situations seem quite tasty. But, unpleasant situations seem tasteless and even bitter and condemnable. Most people just wish for prosperity because they don't have the ability to utilize adversity to their advantage. However, adversity has a most important message and is especially needed for one's evolution.

If you have attained that profound understanding of adversity, you are enriched by both prosperity as well as adversity. Ideally, prosperity should relax your mind so that you turn your gaze towards God, Who is the Source of all prosperity. Similarly, adversity should encourage your mind to reflect. In adversity, you turn away from the world and begin to contemplate within. It is then that you realize you have a Support that has always been present, unlike anything in the world—the Support of the Divine Self, God.

When this realization manifests, you have discovered the Salt of Life, and you are able to relish life even during adversity. That doesn't mean that you should create adversity, but accept adversity and prosperity as they spontaneously and meaningfully occur within your life. Although God's plan is designed for nothing but prosperity, human mind often interprets what is really prosperity as adversity. You may argue, "How can that be? Life is full of problems and worries." The answer is that the human mind perceives circumstances according to ego's values rather than from a higher perspective. Certain situations seem so pleasant and therefore delightful to your ego. Other circumstances are unpleasant to your ego and therefore frustrating. However, in spite of whatever circumstances arise, you will eventually find that the substance of your inner life is empty if you lack aspiration for God-realization. By merely chasing the mirage of pleasure, the Salt, the more profound meaning to your life, will be missing and therefore you will continue to tumble back into this world from one into another.

As you advance and look back, you realize that you owe more to your frustrations than to your prosperity for fortitude and inner enrichment. If you possess that understanding, both prosperity and adversity are viewed as blessings proceeding from God. That understanding is the Salt that flavors everything within your life.

True religion or the spiritual path is the discovery of what immense glory lies within your heart. If ego is not the main focus of your personality, if you enjoy the sweetness of Divine Presence, if your prayer originates from the depth of your heart, if you radiate goodwill and charity around you, then you are a Light placed on a hill. Not only are you a Light to yourself, but a Light to everyone around you. You are the Salt of the Earth. Not only do you "flavor" everything you do for yourself, but the very sight of you becomes "flavorable" for others.

Chapter Fifteen
Faith Can Move Mountains

aith, called *shraddha* in Sanskrit, is the most important virtue to develop as the foundation of your spiritual *sadhana*. If you were to develop true faith, a childlike simplicity would emerge within your personality. For a child, faith is instinctive. A child is not informed about the details or complications of life, not even of the nature of his mother and father; but unconscious faith sustains the child and allows him to be completely relaxed in his home.

You too are sustained by faith in a similar manner. If you lived only by reason, trying to rationally determine where you are going in life and what each day will bring, your mind would explode in a single day. Science tells us that the earth itself is ever tumbling through the vastness of space, the whole universe is expanding, and within it there seems to be an accidental conglomeration of energy and atoms. Thinking about all this, one surely will find it difficult to find any meaning in the world. But look into your heart, and you will see how it beats with the rhythm of faith from your childhood. Indeed, all of nature acts on the basis of such faith.

The simple faith that unfolds in the heart of a truly religious or spiritual person is beautifully expressed in the words of Jesus:

> *Look at the birds in the sky. They don't sow seed or harvest grain or gather crops into barns. Yet your heavenly Father feeds them. Aren't you worth much more than they are? Who among you by worrying can add a single moment to your life? And why do you worry about clothes? Notice how the lilies in the field grow. They don't wear themselves out with work, and they don't spin cloth. But I say to you that even Solomon in all his splendor wasn't dressed like one of these. If God dresses grass in the field so beautifully, even though it's alive today and tomorrow it's thrown into the furnace, won't God do much more for you, you people of weak faith?*
> (CEB Matthew 6:26-30)

Without any egoistic effort, without the help of computers or modern technology, out of the crude earth the lilies have fabricated such wonderful petals. They do not care about the condition of the economy. They have no money in the bank; they do not write notes; they do not hold credit cards. These "illiterate, ignorant beings" bring out such a wonderful expression of beauty. Human perfection with all its glory cannot compare to the perfection that manifests without ego.

If you observe the way in which God's power and intelligence operates behind every little thing in nature, could you not develop that kind of inward trust and feeling? If God has paid so much attention to bringing forth a beautiful lily that is present in the morning and gone by the evening, how much more has He bestowed upon a human being in a human body that is already a profound expression of Divine Art?

Little birds, as well as beasts, ants and butterflies have been cared for in such an amazing way in the universal scheme of life. Therefore, isn't it quite rational to believe that human beings—who are the crown of creation, who possess keen intelligence and such a complex nervous system—must also be supported by that same caring Hand?

Therefore, we must learn profound lessons from the creation—from the sense of freedom expressed by the blossoming flowers and the birds of the air and the fish in the sea. If you learn the art of relaxing the mind even in a world of constant pressure, you are the cleverest human being imaginable!

Although faith is instinctive in everyone, most people, due to mental limitation, are not aware of its power and effectiveness. As you watch your mind, you realize how your faith waivers. Sometimes when you pray and meditate, there is a serene faith; yet at other times when you pray, half your mind is running wild with anxiety. You are praying and at the same time your mind is filled with fear.

It is like the predicament of a child who imagines that there in the corner of his room sits a ghost. Although he holds a flashlight in his hand, he is too afraid to turn it on and see if anything is really there in the corner. Prayer and faith are like that flashlight. Knowing that you have a light in your hand, you should not allow any form of diffidence or fear to exist in any corner of your heart.

When trains first started to run in the villages of India, the villagers entered the train but kept their baggage upon their heads, not understanding that the train would carry the baggage as well as themselves. It took time to introduce them to the fact that the train was carrying everything. Some quickly learned to relax and enjoyed their journey. By the time the others reached their destination, they were exhausted and stressed. Similarly, as you travel through your life in the mighty Divine vehicle of this earth planet, make it your project to discover, strengthen, and enjoy your faith and trust in God.

There is an episode from Indian history about a simple boy who grew to be a powerful seventeenth century Maharasthran king named Shivaji. In the beginning he was a disciple of Sage Samathram Das, who helped him to become a brave and heroic man who subjugated evil forces that threatened society. However, after becoming a king he lost that inner relaxation and began to develop stress in his daily life. He continually thought of the treasury and other royal preoccupations. One day when he was in a miserable state of mind, his Guru noticed him and said, "Let us go for a walk." During the walk his Guru pointed to a rock and said, "Shivaji, pick up that rock and break it open." He did so and a frog that had been hibernating inside the rock emerged. The Guru said, "Look, Shivaji. Who takes care of that frog? Do you?"

The idea behind the anecdote is that even within the most remote and hidden crevasses of the earth, the Divine Hand reaches out and sustains all. So why should you subject yourself to constant stress in life, thinking that you are so important in getting things done? Your ego may react to this, asserting, "If I do not do things, how can faith make them happen?" The fact is that faith does not contradict your self-effort. Complete your responsibilities while promoting happiness, harmony and prosperity—but without stress. If you do so, your self-effort becomes far more productive. On the other hand, when you strive under pressure, your self-effort is quantitative, not qualitative. You may race around accomplishing things, but inwardly you remain hollow.

Where there is faith, there is eternal hope. The Divine is your very essence. God is not an imaginary idea or a concept created out of weakness or convenience. The amazing power of faith has been illustrated again and again throughout history by the lives of great Saints and Sages.

Faith transcends your intellect; but never contradicts it. Faith inspires your intellect to continue to explore in order to authenticate it. Faith moves mountains.

Such faith is not blind, sentimental belief. Faith is not a matter of merely saying, "Yes, I believe in everything that my teacher says. Starting tomorrow I'm going to have intense faith in God or Jesus and thereby be saved forever." Rather, it is the sublime and sincere internal conviction that you are sustained by the Divine Hand at all times, and that that Hand ultimately carries the burden of the world with the most amazing strength and wisdom.

Faith must be cultivated gradually, day by day, as you harmonize your personality through Integral Yoga. As you succeed in this effort, faith enables you to attune yourself with nature. You realize that the same Hand that allows the lilies to bloom, that shines through the sun and the moon is behind your pulsating heart. You are always in God. With this understanding life becomes inspiring. Little by little you shed your burden, remove your complexes, and break the fetters that have confined you. Day by day you discover yourself becoming more and more emancipated. Life lived with faith is the life of true religion, the life of great joy.

Chapter Sixteen

The Sublime
Thread of Prayer

Prayer is the subtlest and most sublime thread that links the human soul with the Divine Spirit. It is a golden bridge that establishes a relationship between the finite individual and the Infinite Supreme. It is the winged arrow of human feeling that unites with the Divine Love of God. It is the spark of light that glows within a pure heart expanding into a florescent luminosity. It is the cool breeze that blows from the Ocean of Love into the arid life of man.

There is no religion that does not expound the glory of prayer. There is no Saint who did not take recourse to prayer in their spiritual movement. There is no great being upon this earth who did not offer prayers at the recognition of the Divine Hand guiding the mysterious world to mystic ends.

For many, however, prayer becomes merely a repetition of hymns or words. Real prayer does not depend upon how many beautiful words you have selected to repeat constantly. It should not be merely lip service or an ostentatious ritual. As Lord Jesus urged His disciples:

*... **when thou prayest, enter into thy closet, and when thou hast shut thy door, pray to thy Father that which is in secret; and thy Father which seeth in secret shall reward thee openly.*** (KJ21 Matthew 6:6)

God responds not so much to your external display, but to the feeling that flows within your heart. What you offer to God in secret, God accepts; but if you offer it ostentatiously, God shies away.

To be truly prayerful, develop a childlike simplicity. Just as a child runs to his mother with absolute trust, you must be able to run to the loving Presence of God with a spirit of resignation and profound yearning.

The power of prayer depends upon the purity of your feeling, which must become free from egocentricities, untarnished by greed, anger, hatred, pride and gross sentiments. To be truly effective, prayer requires liberation from personal prejudices and limitations caused by gross feelings and erroneous functions of the mind. Most importantly, it depends on the intensity of your yearning to unite yourself with the Supreme Self within—your yearning to lead your soul to the transcendent planes of Spirit where time becomes a myth, where changes cease to operate, where mortality evaporates like darkness vanishing before light, where pain terminates and sorrow exists no more.

Every religion encompasses prayers revealed by great Sages and Saints that express lofty ideas and thoughts. However, if you repeat them mechanically without focusing on the beauty and grandeur of the meaning and the feeling, they are not as effective as they could be.

There is a famous prayer from Brihadaranyaka Upanishad:

Asato Ma Sad Gamaya;
Tamaso Ma Jyotir Gamaya;
Mrityor Ma Amritam Gamaya.

"Lead me from unreal to real;
Lead me from darkness to light;
Lead me from death to immortality."

This prayer beckons the aspirant to recognize within the depths of his heart the presence of Divinity in the form of Truth that abides forever, Light that is pure transcendental wisdom, and Immortality that is the state of communion with the Divinity.

Similarly, there is a Vedic prayer called Gayatri Mantra:

Om Bhur Bhuvah Swah
Tat Savitur Varenyam
Bhargo Devasya Dheemahi
Dhiyo Yo Nah Pracho Dayaat.

"Om. We adore that *Brahman*, the Supreme Self,
Who, like the sun, illumines the three planes—
physical, astral and causal.
May He enlighten our intellect."

Buddhism has a well-known prayer that emphasizes the dedication of human will to the transcendental will of the Cosmic Being.:

Buddham Sharanam Gachhami.
Dharmam Sharanam Gachhami.
Sangham Sharanam Gachhami.

"I take refuge in Buddha, the enlightened;
I take refuge in *dharma*, the spiritual law;
I take refuge in the Order."

Christians recite the Lord's Prayer:

Our Father Who art in Heaven,
Hallowed be Thy Name.
Thy Kingdom come.
Thy will be done on earth,
As it is in Heaven.
Give us this day our daily bread
And forgive us our trespasses,
As we forgive those who trespass against us.

And lead us not into temptation,
But deliver us from evil:
For Thine is the Kingdom, the Power,
And the Glory
Forever and ever
Amen

This prayer, which is highlighted in the next chapter, asks man to recognize the presence of God in day-to-day life and to dedicate his individual will to the Supreme. Sins are not mere violations of moral laws; they originate from the ignorance of one's spiritual nature. Therefore, the eagerness not to sin implies aspiration for communion with God through wisdom, through devotion and through sublime actions.

Thus every prayer demands faith, devotion to God, sincerity of aspiration, integration of one's personality, and affirmation of the Spirit within. With feeling and understanding, every prayer, no matter from what religion or sect, becomes powerful and dynamic. But without meaning and feeling, every religious prayer, no matter how beautifully fashioned, no matter how sublimely written, no matter how clearly expressed, becomes like a lifeless repetition of recorded sounds.

Begin praying according to your deeper feelings and inclinations. As you pray, feel the presence of the Lord—a feeling so beautifully highlighted in the words of Alfred Lord Tennyson:

Speak to Him, thou, for He heareth,
And spirit with Spirit can meet,
Nearer is He than breathing,
Closer than hands and feet.

And when you have finished your prayers, practice virtue in your day-to-day activities. The spirit of prayerfulness should permeate every good action, making that action itself a form of prayer to the Divine within. If your actions are tainted by greed, deception and cruelty, your prayers are merely words of vanity and hypocrisy.

As the flood-gates of feeling open in your heart, you will find that words cease and your sentiment for God continues to flow on uninterruptedly, whether you are working or resting, whether you are walking or sitting. Only then has prayer assumed a more intense form. It is this all-engulfing, all-absorbing, and all-purifying stream of prayer that can overcome all degrading inclinations of the soul and lead it to the state of its innermost beauty and glory.

Chapter Seventeen
The Lord's Prayer

Our Father Who art in Heaven,
Hallowed be Thy Name.
Thy Kingdom come.
Thy will be done on earth,
As it is in Heaven.
Give us this day our daily bread
And forgive us our trespasses,
As we forgive those who trespass against us.
And lead us not into temptation,
But deliver us from evil:
For Thine is the Kingdom, the Power,
And the Glory
Forever and ever
Amen

The importance of prayer is recognized in every religious and spiritual system of the world. It is the most effective means of elevating the mind and

raising the level of one's consciousness to the lofty heights of heavenly glory.

In the Yogic tradition, prayer is practiced in many forms:

1. Verbal prayer according to one's choice.
2. Chanting or reciting scriptural prayers composed by great Sages and Saints.
3. *Japa* or the repetition of mantra (the Divine Name in the form of sacred mystic formulas).
4. *Kirtan* or singing the Divine Name or the glories of God.
5. Repetition of mantra along with devout meditation on the many attributes of God.
6. Allowing the mind to flow toward God in silent meditation.
7. Awareness of Divine Presence and total surrender to God.

In the light of these points, let us study the Lord's Prayer:

Our Father Who art in Heaven, hallowed be Thy Name.

The repetition of Divine Name is the mystical art of glorifying God, His Name, and the Divine qualities implied within that Name. It is also the easiest method of reaching out to God.

The various Sanskrit mantras, the Names of God, are the glorification of the different aspects of the Divinity. Choose a Divine Name that inspires you and repeat it with the help of a *mala* (rosary). Along with every repetition, feel that you are being enfolded by the Presence of God. By constant practice, by constantly calling out to God, a Divine association is generated between the unconscious mind and the mantra, the Name of God. Therefore, when the mantra is recited, the unconscious awakens lofty impressions and a Divine Presence manifests.

Similarly, you may sing the Name of God and thus practice *kirtan*. Any prayer, mantra or Name of God adapted to music or chanted becomes *kirtan*. Set aside a selected period of time during the day (preferably in the early morning) when you can practice *japa* or *kirtan* intensively for half an hour or more. Then, your daily duties are performed with a mind filled with the sublimity of spiritual vibrations.

As you advance, the sense of prayerfulness and the awareness of Divine Presence should permeate your entire existence. A sweet stream of Divine remembrance should continue to flow deep within your heart at all times: while walking, sitting, resting, talking, sleeping—even during the difficult challenges of life.

Thy Kingdom come. Thy will be done on earth, as it is in Heaven.

As the practice of prayerfulness advances, you will begin to see the Hand of God behind every development in your life and the world around you. At first you feel the Divine Presence in the glorious objects of the world—you see the effulgence of God shining in the sun, His bliss radiating through the moon, His fullness surging in the ocean. Thus, you see the glory of God permeating all the objects that inspire your mind.

Next you begin to feel the Divine Presence even behind objects that are generally disliked: hurricanes and earthquakes, snakes and scorpions, diseases and adversities. In this state, you enjoy absolute surrender to the Divine Will. You become an instrument in Divine Hands, asserting, "Thy Will be done."

Finally, the pinnacle of this spiritual vision is the realization, "All this is nothing but God Himself." It is then that Heaven is brought down to this earth. Divine Consciousness is realized even in one's limited personality. This ideal is expressed in the Upanishadic peace chant:

Om poornam-adah poornam-idam
poornaat poornam-udachyate.
Poornasya poornam-aadaaya
poornam-evaavashishyate.
Om Shaantih Shaantih Shaantih

"*Om*, That (Divine Self) is Full; and this (the world, which is nothing but God manifesting through Cosmic Illusion) is also Full.

When this world (of illusory names and forms)
is negated (by transcending it through Self-
realization),what is left is Full (the Divine Self).
Let there be Peace! Peace! Peace!"

When you advance on the spiritual path leading
to the realization of this mystic Fullness, you
continue to be a source of increasing peace and
harmony for the world around you. You become a
Cosmic benefactor and thus, figuratively speaking,
bring Heaven upon the earth.

Give us this day our daily bread
and forgive us our trespasses as
we forgive those who trespass against us.

The message of this stanza focuses the mind on
the present day and its realities. Mental energy that
is spent dwelling on negative memories of the past
and worrying about the future is wasted in vain.
Develop a sense of dynamic contentment with your
"daily bread," that is, the realities and duties of daily
life, and accept them as a gift from God.

Also, life in this relative world must be lived to
fulfill the fivefold debts:

1. Debt to God, paid by the practice of prayer,
meditation and other devotional exercises.
2. Debt to the Sages and Saints, paid by studying
their spiritual works and following their
teachings.

3. Debt to one's forefathers, paid by promoting righteous conduct in life that brings glory and fame to the family in which one is born.
4. Debt to human beings, paid by serving them in various selfless ways.
5. Debt to animals, paid by being kind and compassionate towards all living creatures.

For whatever imperfections may exist in the proper fulfillment of these debts, seek the forgiveness of God. In turn, develop the quality of forgiveness towards others. To the extent you forgive another and have the capacity to understand them lovingly, to that extent you become the recipient of Divine Grace and forgiveness.

✧ And lead us not into temptation, ✧ but deliver us from evil.

According to Yoga philosophy, the source of evil is *avidya* or ignorance, which is the lack of awareness of one's Divine Identity. When ignorance is removed by the intuitive knowledge that "I Am One with God," you become a *Jivan Mukta*—one liberated in life. This is the very goal that is sought through this prayer to God.

That which leads you away from the path to Self-realization—God—is called temptation. Numerous temptations are arrayed before every individual. As an aspirant you learn to turn away from what is merely and apparently "pleasant" and direct your steps towards what is truly "good."

By developing constant devotion to God, you draw inner spiritual strength that helps you transform the manifold expressions of lust, greed and anger (the "triple gates to hell"). But those who lack devotion continue to be led astray, distracted by the numerous temptations of the world.

✐✄ For Thine is the Kingdom, the Power and ✄✐ the Glory, forever and ever. Amen.

The development of supreme dispassion implies that you are so inspired to become one with God that temptations for earth's worldly pleasures fade in comparison. When you discover the Kingdom of Heaven within your very heart, you abide in God forever. Nothing is impossible. With the assistance of the boundless power and glory of God, you have crossed the ocean of the world-process and will never return to it again.

"Amen" is a mystical word—a modification of *Om*, which symbolizes *Brahman* or the Absolute Self. The power of prayer is enhanced by the repetition of the sacred formula *Om* (or Amen). When the spirit of prayer rises to its fullness, the world of multiplicity is effaced. God alone remains the Truth that was, is and ever shall be!

Chapter Eighteen
An Insight into Miracles

Great miraculous occurrences continue to manifest before you—internally and externally. When you develop a mind that is saturated in Divine Love, you are aware of the sweetness of the Divine Presence; you begin to commune with the blessings and miracles of the Universe. In other words, you sense the workings of faith; you realize that Celestial Grace works wonders. You experience the effulgent presence of God within you and in others, like the luminous sun pouring through a window.

The human mind has always been fascinated by miracles, and most people experience a miraculous development at sometime during their life. There are people who even believe that one can miraculously attain Enlightenment. Therefore, it is important to understand what a miracle is and is not.

The miracle of Moses parting the sea

All religious history abounds with miracles. Some of these are vivid and extremely impressive to the mind. Recall how Moses, for example, was leading his people to freedom when the pharaoh proceeded to march against them. Moses turned to God and a miracle occurred: The Red Sea parted, allowing the people following Moses to escape. By the miracles of Lord Jesus, the blind began to see, the lame began to walk, and a dead man even came to life. In the Ramayana, Saint Tulsidasji offered prayers to God stating, *"Mooka hoy bachaal, pangu chadhai girivar gahan"*—"By Your grace one who is dumb becomes an eloquent speaker, and one who is lame climbs an inaccessible mountain."

To the sensitive eye, every tiny or grand thing in this entire creation is a miraculous expression of the Divine Self. Wherever you look, there are miracles. See how, from a tiny, infinitesimal seed there emerges a tender sprout, and that sprout in the course of time grows into a gigantic and stately tree. How, out of crude earth, does a tree through the use of a complicated chemical arrangement of molecules manifest such magnificence? See how a flower unfolds its beauty and fragrance, creating a delicious nectarine fruit to nourish and delight us. See how a human being grows from conception to old age, how the intelligent systems of your own body perform all their complex missions to maintain your life. See how the birds migrate. Think of how they are all united and led in unison back to their original location thousands of miles away without maps, without a compass, without the study of latitude and longitude. All these are amazing miracles.

In addition to the grand miracle of this whole creation, there are exceptional miracles experienced by people who are spiritually sensitive and who are following the path to God-realization. These specialized miracles are like the ignition generated by sunlight focused through a magnifying glass. Although sunlight is generally diffused, it creates a spark when the rays have been concentrated by the lens. So too, Divine miracles are everywhere, but when one's mind is purified and focused, those miracles become apparent.

To understand the role of miracles in one's life, it is important to understand that nothing happens unless it is in accordance with one's karma, the law of cause and effect, the law of action and its reaction. Nothing takes place unless you deserve it by your self-effort, whether it is something miraculous or something perfectly normal.

If you have qualified yourself, things may indeed happen to you in a miraculous way in the Divine Plan. However, if you are not prepared for Enlightenment, if you are not deserving of higher knowledge, then it is a great folly to think that one day you will meet a Sage who will miraculously place his hand right on your head and cause your inner eye to burst forth, allowing you to soar into Enlightenment.

The Miracle of the Cloth

One evening, St. Peter entered a village and knocked at the door of a wealthy lady. "Who is there?" asked the lady. St. Peter replied, "I am a stranger. I would like to rest for a while and have a little food and drink. I am very tired, hungry and thirsty."

The lady shut the door in his face and said, "I do not have the time or the interest in giving you all that. Why should I help those who are lazy and who do not work for themselves? Whatever wealth I have attained I have worked for. You can't share my wealth just by knocking at my door, so go your own way!"

Peter went on his way and knocked at the door of a poor lady who spun cloth and sold it at the market. When she opened the door, he again asked for a little food, drink and a bit of time to rest. She welcomed him in, saying, "I am very poor. However, whatever I have I will share with you. There is nothing more delightful than sharing what I have with someone."

St. Peter was very pleased. He ate the food, rested and then departed. But before leaving he blessed the lady, saying, "Tomorrow, the first job that you perform will continue until the end of that day." Although the lady couldn't understand what these words meant, she thanked him graciously.

The next day, the lady was planning her projects for the day, and the idea to measure the cloth that she had previously spun came to her mind. She then took a yardstick and started unrolling and measuring her cloth. Lo and behold, because of the boon St. Peter had given her, the cloth went on multiplying from morning 'til night! To her amazement, it produced cartload after cartload of the most extraordinary fabric with the most unique design. The next day when the lady took the cartloads of cloth to market, everything was sold. She earned so much money that she never again had to worry about her wellbeing.

During the time that the poor lady was measuring the amazing extensions of cloth, the rich lady who had turned St. Peter away happened to pass by. Awed by the huge quantities of beautiful and costly cloth, she said, "How did you acquire all that?" "Well," replied the poor lady, "I had a guest yesterday who gave me a strange boon before he left." As she described the guest and his visit, the rich lady realized that it was the very same man whom she had turned away from her own door. Cunningly, the rich lady then said, "The next time he comes around, send him to me. You will be doing him a great favor because I will give him much better food than you could ever give him."

To be sure that she would get the same blessing that the poor lady had received, she placed the most costly fabric possible in her living room, ready to be rolled out and measured. Then day after day she waited for St. Peter to arrive.

Finally one day, St. Peter knocked on her door. With a great hypocritical show of joy, she welcomed him into her home and served him all types of rich food. When he had eaten and was ready to leave, she said, "Please give me the same boon that you gave to the other lady in this village who fed you." St. Peter replied, "I will give you the same boon: Tomorrow, the first work that you do will continue until the end of that day." She said, "Very well, nothing more do I ask." Thus saying, St. Peter went on his way.

The next day, when the lady was about to start her project of measuring and thus multiplying the cloth, she suddenly became thirsty. The idea came into her mind that she must have water nearby while she worked. So she went to the well and began drawing water. Since that was her first activity of the day, in accordance with the boon, it continued throughout that day without stopping. So much water cascaded out of the well that by the afternoon it had reached her neck. By evening the water had reached her nose. She shouted for help, but no one came to rescue her. By sundown her whole body was overwhelmed with the deluge and she finally drowned.

This simple parable conveys a great message. The lady whose heart was filled with generosity and simplicity experienced a miracle of continuous prosperity. Like that lady, you are always spinning a fabric—the fabric of your karma. If you are a devotee of God, if you are generous, simple, and loving, your good karma will go on multiplying day by day. By "sundown," by the time you are ready to depart from this earth, your mind will be so filled with Divine impressions and backed up by such an abundance of Divine Grace that you will not return to the world again. You will attain the Kingdom of Heaven, Enlightenment, Liberation.

On the other hand, if you are hypocritical, greedy, and egocentric, there is another type of miracle waiting for you. You go on creating a flood of karmas that "drown" your opportunity to reach the Kingdom of Heaven. These impressions carry you back to earth to be born again until you learn the glory of loving God and being generous towards your fellow man, which then reawakens your opportunity and brings you to the gates of Liberation.

To be receptive to miracles requires that your mind be charged with devotion to God. If you are living your life well by utilizing your energy for the good of others as well as for yourself, then you will begin to see Divine miracles occurring in your life. You will be amazed to discover a world of unique beauty and glory not obvious to ordinary minds, and you will begin to feel the Hand of Infinite Compassion sustaining you in every situation.

The culmination of all miraculous experiences is the attainment of God-realization. Is it not the most amazing miracle that a soul can come into the world as a human being, share so many of the characteristics of the animal world, and rise to the level of Godhood? To be immersed in the Divine Self, to become Saintly and waft the aroma of eternity, to be forever free of the cycles of birth and death is indeed the Miracle of all miracles!

Mysticism of the Miracles of Lord Jesus

Except ye see signs and wonders,
ye will not believe.
(KJV St. John 4:48)

For those who are spiritually advanced, the world pulsates with Divine Glory. There is a miracle at every step. However, those who have not developed subtlety of reason and purity of feeling need to experience grosser miracles to believe according to their egoistic concepts. Saints and Sages have worked miracles to instill faith in the human heart. However, their miracles are not confined to curing diseases and healing the handicapped. Their miracles are meant to cure the root disease of ignorance, and to heal the sickness of the world-process.

According to the Vedantic text, Yoga Vasistha, ignorance is the root disease that prevents you from witnessing the nature of Self. Your Divine Self is, so

to speak, hidden from your view. Due to this disease, the unconscious becomes conditioned by increasing impressions of attachment and hatred towards objects, people and circumstances. A diseased mind is unable to experience the freedom of lofty thoughts and expansive feelings because of the cobwebs of illusion woven by an egoistic vision.

The disease of the mind (*adhi*) gives rise to the imbalance in the flow of vitality in the physical body resulting in the development of physical diseases. Therefore, to cure the diseases of the body and mind, you must witness the signs and wonders— the miracles—of the Divine Self operating within your personality.

As spiritual consciousness unfolds within your heart, you witness great miracles within your personality and within the personalities of others. Christ, who dwells within every being, begins to perform amazing works of Divine glory. The blindness of attachment is healed. Thus, the blind see. A lame person is one who is unable to perform self-effort due to the pressure of negative karmas from the past. Thus, under the Divine influence of Jesus, the lame walk again. Craving afflicts the soul like leprosy, and robs it of its vital limbs. Thus, Christ's love heals that affliction. The souls suffering from the palsy of greed are freed from the disease of deep-rooted selfishness. The dumbness of inertia is cured, and the soul becomes eloquent in expressing the glory of the Divine Self.

Worldly miseries are symbolized by a burning fever. With increasing spiritual sensitivity, even the pleasures of the world are understood to be modifications of pain, because whatever joy exists in those pleasures eventually fades. One is again left wondering how to finally attain the ultimate happiness. Spiritual maturity cures you of this burning fever, replacing it with a more sublime form of joy. The soul is led to the gardens of spiritual expansion wherein the breeze of peace removes its fever forever. Finally, the very root of evil—ignorance—is removed from your soul by the mere command of Christ. Divine insight tears the veil of ignorance by its mere glance.

By seeing the wonders of spiritual movement, you develop profound faith in the Divine Self. Within your heart, faith blooms into the realization that you have attained the Kingdom of Heaven.

The Miracle of the Loaves and Fishes

In Luke 9: 13-17, it is told that five thousand men who were following Jesus needed to be given something to eat, but His disciples were at a loss about how they were going to feed all of them with only five loaves of bread and two fishes. Without any hesitation, Jesus had his followers sit down. Then He blessed the loaves and fish and kept breaking them

into pieces until all the hungry had been fed. When everyone had eaten to full satisfaction, Jesus asked His disciples to gather up the leftovers, which were enough to fill twelve baskets.

Mystically, five thousand men symbolize the world of multiplicity revealed by the five senses. Hunger operating at the level of the senses is unappeasable even by all the objects of the world. In other words, no matter what wealth and prosperity one acquires in the world, the soul remains hungry. One continues to look for fulfillment.

However, with increasing spiritual advancement, the clamorous cravings represented by the hunger of five thousand men are gradually and fully satisfied by the subtle taste of spiritual Bliss. A spiritual aspirant gathers up the fragments of the mind through a spiritual feast represented by the "five loaves" (purification of the senses) and "two fishes" (purification of the intellect and ego). Spontaneously, *vairagya* (dispassion) toward the acquisitions of the world unfolds.

The Miracle of the Resurrection of Lazarus

In NIV John 11: 41–44, the events surrounding the death and resurrection of Lazarus are beautifully described. This gospel tells how Jesus traveled into the country of Jordan after escaping from those who were enraged because He had proclaimed His

Divine identity. There He received the message from Mary and Martha, two sisters of Lazarus and devotees of Jesus, that Lazarus was sick and near death. When Jesus arrived four days later, however, Lazarus had already died and his body had been placed in a tomb. Intending to reveal the glory of God operating through Him, Jesus removed the rock at the entrance to the tomb and prayed to His heavenly father: *"Father, I thank you that you have heard me. I knew that you always hear me, but I said this for the benefit of the people standing here, that they may believe that you sent me."* When He had said this, Jesus called in a loud voice, *"Lazarus, come out!"* To the astonishment of many who had assembled to see this miracle, the dead man came out, his hands and feet wrapped with strips of linen and a cloth around his face. Jesus said to them, "Take off the grave clothes and let him go."

Lazarus is symbolic of the human soul caught in the clutches of death. Attachment, hatred, pride, egoism, greed, craving, fear, sorrow and grief—all these are the clutches of death. Ignorance is the sickness that deprives the soul of the Truth that it is essentially immortal. This ignorance drives the soul to a state of "death"—to reincarnate again and again, life after life. When the soul is unable to discover this hidden Truth and release itself from the bondage of the world-process, it is, as it were, dead. The Divine

Movement symbolized by Jesus must awaken the soul from its slumber of death.

Mary and Martha are symbolic of the two paths: *Shreya* (the path of blessedness through inward spiritual movement), and *preya* (the path of pleasure through outgoing movement in the material world). They are sisters of the soul, because they intend to aid the soul in its journey towards the Divine Resurrection—the state of Self-realization. However, it is Mary whose love of Jesus is all-effacing and profound.

Elsewhere in the Bible (Luke 10: 38-42), the symbolism of Mary and Martha is clarified through a parable. Jesus was once received by both sisters, but while Mary went and sat down at the feet of Jesus, her sister Martha continued to trouble herself by arranging and fixing her house in order to show respect for Jesus. Jesus pointed out that between these two sisters, Mary had made the better choice. While the outgoing movement of the mind (Martha) continues to look after the transient developments of the world in the name of adoring the Divine Self, the internalized movement of mind (Mary) moves directly to the Divine Self through the power of intuition and devotion. Therefore, it is better to befriend the "Mary" aspect of one's mind in order to be resurrected from "death" (individualized consciousness backed up ignorance).

Converting Water into Wine

In John 2:1-11, it is told that once Jesus and His disciples attended a marriage ceremony in Galilee. When they asked for some wine, they were told by Mary, the mother of Jesus, that there was no wine to be had. Jesus then instructed the servants to take six empty kegs and fill them to the brim with water. When the governor of the feast was served a drink from the kegs, he joyously praised the bridegroom for serving his very best wine to his guests. This miracle performed by Lord Jesus demonstrated before the eyes of His disciples the glory of His Divine power and intensified their belief in His identity as the Enlightened Messiah.

The symbolism of marriage in spiritual literature always implies the wedding of the soul to its essential Self. Life in pursuit of spiritual advancement is not a process of pathetic austerity. Rather, it is a procession of Divine festivity. But when the intoxicating "wine" of spiritual devotion is lacking, this marriage becomes a process of humiliation and pain.

The kegs are human personalities. The vital forces operating through the body are represented by the water. When spiritual initiation instills Divine aspiration in the human personality, the water turns into wine, as it were. Mother Mary symbolizes Mother Nature, Prakriti, who arranges the feast of the world-process. It is by Her intervention that the

Divine Self converts the "water" of physical life (the vital forces) into the "wine" of spiritual life.

The Miracle of Spiritual Transformation

While visiting His native land of Nazareth, Jesus went to the synagogue, according to the custom, and gave a sermon, reading from the old texts of the Bible. He spoke about how the prophecies of ancient times had been fulfilled through His personality. This greatly irritated the people of His native land. They could not believe that one among them, a mere carpenter's son, could rise to such lofty heights of spiritual consciousness and then declare it. They intended to destroy Him by throwing Him off a towering cliff. However, Jesus quietly went on His way after stating, *"A prophet hath no honor in his own country."* (KJV John 4:44)

The mystic implication of this episode is very profound. Spiritual movement is characterized by a series of transformations. A caterpillar is transformed into a butterfly. Thus transformed, it no longer belongs to the family and the homeland of the caterpillars. It flies away, enjoying the beauty and elegance of many gardens, something it never would have imagined had it remained a caterpillar.

In the same way, aspirants begin as caterpillars. They have no idea what sublime spiritual gardens await them through the exalted advancement of the soul. In the beginning, they only know Caterpillar

Ville. Following the path of spiritual movement, they become witnesses to the glorious miracles of the Divine Self operating through them. They realize that all prophecies were symbolic statements referring to the Truth of the Self that lies within. Spiritual forecasts presented by great prophets were not referring to historical developments in time and space, but to the understanding of the utmost unfolding of Divine potentiality that exists within every man and woman.

The inhabitants of Nazareth misinterpreted this affirmation of fulfillment within the soul of man. They mistakenly thought this Divine Truth to be an egoistic statement of blasphemy. The cause of their misunderstanding was their familiarity with Jesus. They could not outgrow their old concepts to see who He was in the present moment. It is important for an aspirant to outgrow meaningless concepts on the spiritual path. The movement should be from the known to the unknown, from the relative world of multiplicity to the transcendental realm of Nonduality. Nonduality is an unknown territory for an aspirant. This great need for adjusting to the ever-new vision arising from the soul must be recognized, lest the atmosphere of contempt based upon familiarity ousts the "Jesus" in man. However, it is impossible to throw Jesus off the cliff—to remove Him from one's consciousness. He continues to move on in spiritual silence.

Chapter Nineteen

Celebration of the Spirit

The Birth, Crucifixion and Resurrection of Divine Jesus

The biblical story of the life of Lord Jesus, from His birth to His resurrection, has been a source of the greatest devotional inspiration for millions of worshippers. Devout Christians and even people of other faiths rejoice during the Christmas and Easter seasons, commemorating the birth of Christ, His miraculous acts, His wondrous teachings, His crucifixion, and His resurrection. These mystic events are celebrated with church services, delightfully adorned homes, an abundance of light-filled decorations, singing of devotional songs and hymns, festive meals, and the sharing of gifts with loved ones and those in need.

Similarly, in countries around the world, events in the lives of other Divine incarnations, Sages, and men and women of great spiritual significance are celebrated with immense joy and devotion. For example, the life of Lord Krishna is colorfully portrayed in the Hindu scripture known as Srimad Bhagavatam, and his birth is celebrated with one of the biggest religious festivals in the world. To devotees, *Janmashtami* is Christmas and New Year's in one celebration, a day of deep spiritual renewal. Very much like Christmas festivities, it is celebrated with scriptural readings in the temples, colorful decorations and garlands, the singing of devotional *kirtans*, waving of light, delicious feasts and giving gifts to the Lord. The festivities begin before dawn and extend all day until midnight—the time, according to the scriptural stories, that Lord Krishna—like Christ—was born.

The stories contained in the Holy Bible and Srimad Bhagavatam have brought us inspiring portraits of Christ and Krishna as amazing historical personalities that have transformed the world and inspired the greatest realization of human potential. However, Sages remind us that all religious scriptures are actually allegorical in nature, and history is not the most important, inspiring, or transformative aspect of their teachings. A greater reward awaits us if we look into the symbolic meaning of the scriptural accounts to discover and deeply understand the profound meaning of the teachings.

Every festival in an advanced religious system is based upon the commemoration of spiritual or mystical events. Behind every holy day, what is really being celebrated is the ancient theme of the victory of Light over darkness. The spirit has, as it were, battled against the forces of darkness from time immemorial and has proven its supremacy over matter again and again. This is what is symbolized in every religious festival. Highly evolved beings from various religions of the world have presented this fact symbolically in the form of stories about Avatars, Sages, Saints and others who have engaged in this ancient battle.

Lord Jesus—the Divine Avatara

The role of Lord Jesus, seen through the eyes of the Vedic mind, is the role of an *Avatara*, an incarnation of God. Jesus says, *"Come to me, all you who labor and are heavy laden, and I will give you rest."* (NKJV Matthew 11:28) The "me" He was referring to is the Universal Self. Much in the same way, in the Gita, Lord Krishna says, "Whosoever surrenders to me will be free of all limitations and attain Liberation."

Reflect, too, on the following quotation from the Old Testament:

> *And Moses said unto God, "Behold, when I come unto the children of Israel, and shall say unto them, 'The God of your fathers*

hath sent me unto you', and they shall say to me, "What is his name?" What shall I say unto them?" And God said unto Moses, "I AM THAT I AM." And He said, "Thus shalt thou say unto the children of Israel, 'I Am hath sent me unto you.'"
(KJV Exodus 3:13-14)

The "I Am" of Lord Jesus is the "I Am" that was declared by God to Moses in the Old Testament. So when Jesus refers to Himself, He is not referring to His historical personality, although His historical personality is a wonderful symbol of that Absolute Self. *"Before Abraham was, I Am."* (KJV John 8:58) This statement makes it clear that Jesus is not referring to His own personality as the son of Joseph and Mary, for how could He have existed before Mary and Abraham? That "I Am" in Him is the eternal "I Am"—one's essential identity as *Brahman* the Absolute—which is known when one attains Enlightenment or what Lord Jesus refers to as the Kingdom of Heaven.

Although the Divine Incarnation of Jesus is very similar to the concept of *Avatara* (Divine Descent) in the Vedic culture, there is an interesting difference. In Christianity, Jesus appeared only once and will manifest again only on the final Day of Judgment. In Vedic culture, the Divine Self, the *Avatara*, continues to manifest again and again in every *yuga* or age. Christian thought views time as linear and, therefore, does not promote the idea of repeated incarnations of Christ. Vedic thought, on the other hand, sees time as an eternally cyclical process that is more favorable to the idea of repeated incarnations of God. Thus, Rama, Christ, Krishna and others will manifest again and again (under different names) to relieve the earth of the burden of unrighteousness and to promote the path of godliness.

It is easy, however, for a thoughtful aspirant to understand that both the Christian and Vedic concepts of *Avatara* are relative in nature. To a person whose mind is steeped in devotion, this world is an expression of Divinity. Therefore, the Divine Self perpetually manifests for that devotee. The Divinity is here and now, transcending all relative concepts of time and space.

Therefore, it is not necessary to establish the historical authenticity of the details of the lives of Christ, Buddha, Rama or Krishna, or to accept or reject their miraculous deeds. These renowned spiritual beings—symbolic of the Spiritual Consciousness in man—exist always. They existed in the past and will continue to exist in the future, because they are the Reality transcending the limitations of the human mind.

From a more philosophical point of view, every human bei ng and their life on earth has a universal meaning. Therefore, that life can be understood

on a more profound and symbolic level. While the profundity and glory of universal life is less perceptible for the majority of people, it is as visible as the blazing sun to spiritually evolved beings such as Christ, Buddha, Krishna or Rama. Therefore, one can clearly see the spiritual journey of the soul, a journey that is the ultimate destination of every person on earth, reflected in the life of Christ. The sufferings of the limited soul, its aspiration for attaining God-realization, the stairways of spiritual evolution on which the human consciousness must ascend, the challenging obstructions that it courageously faces and surmounts, the glorious vistas of transcendental Consciousness that it will encounter on its march towards God, the magnificent transformations that it undergoes, the sublime and glorious Bliss and peace that it will ultimately realize—all these are reflected in the life and teachings of Christ, as well as in all great spiritual personalities who are adored in the various religions.

In this spirit, let us explore the mystic symbolism implied by the birth, crucifixion, and resurrection of Christ in the light of the philosophy of Vedanta.

The Birth of Lord Jesus

Saint Matthew provides a quote from the prophet Isaiah: *"Behold, a virgin shall be with child, and shall bring forth a son, and they shall call his name Emmanuel, which being interpreted is, God with us."* (KJV Matthew 1:23) When Mary, who was betrothed to Joseph, was pregnant, a Divine angel informed Joseph that Mary was to bring forth the Son of God named Jesus. Thus, the ancient prophecy was to be fulfilled.

Before the birth, Joseph and Mary had left Galilee and traveled to Bethlehem, the City of David, because Christ was from the house and family of David. Christ was born there in Bethlehem in the middle of the night in a manger, because the local inn did not have a room available. Surrounding Him were simple shepherds that had come to rejoice at the birth.

Lord Jesus was born when Herod was king. Herod was terribly afraid that the old prophecy (KJV Psalm 2:6 and Zechariah 9:9) might be fulfilled in Christ, and that Christ might usurp his kingdom and power. Therefore, he sent three wise men from the East to go to Jerusalem to identify the child. When the three wise men arrived, guided by the Eastern Star, they worshiped Jesus and offered gifts of gold, frankincense, and myrrh. However, they did not return to Herod since they understood his intention, but instead departed for their own country. This event was soon followed by the cruel massacre of children ordered by Herod, and the child Jesus was taken to Egypt for safety.

Mystic Symbolism of Christ's Birth

The Spirit must manifest its glory through every human being. When spiritual aspiration dawns deep within the unconscious, Christ is born in the depths of one's being. However, in the state of ignorance, the inner depths of one's personality are dingy and dark. Midnight is suggestive of the serene and silent hours of internalization that bring about the birth of spiritual aspiration. Only those who are "simple" due to lack of egoistic complexes and "childlike" due to purity recognize the birth of Christ. As a result of many good karmas of the past, an inner mystical movement commences in the life of an aspirant. This esoteric movement, characterized by growing aspiration, is the birth of Christ and will eventually grow into Christ Consciousness.

Bethlehem, the city of David, is symbolic of the purified heart of man wherein Christ is born. The inn represents an externalized mind wherein diverse thoughts of sense objects come and go. Desires, sentiments, worldly expectations and ambitions all abound in the inn. On the other hand, the manger symbolizes the internalized mind wherein the thought-waves are withdrawn. There one finds profound serenity and simplicity. The Divine birth in man is softer than the blossoming of a rose in the hours of the night, and yet its implications are more deafening than the clapping of thunder.

The Sages or three wise men from the East are led by a Celestial Star that proclaims the birth of the Child and the place in which He was born. This is the star of insight, born of faith, which discerns the spiritual birth in human personality, even in the depths of the dark unconscious.

Having discovered the Baby, the Sages bestow lavish gifts. The three wise men are symbolic of the three modes of Nature or *gunas* of Prakriti: *sattwa* (purity), *rajas* (activity) and *tamas* (inertia). Their gifts represent the sublime functions of these three modes of Nature. When desires and the subconscious complexes imprison the spirit in man, Nature cannot offer its most bounteous wealth. Instead, Nature robs people of their vitality, intelligence and power. But in the case of Christ, Nature is well pleased and offers its finest and choicest gifts to help the soul discover its essential glory.

The gift of gold is symbolic of *sattwa* or spiritual purity. Frankincense is symbolic of *rajas*, and symbolizes Divine expansion and expressions of virtue wafting a heavenly aroma. Myrrh represents a gum-like substance, which is symbolic of *tamas* or inertia because of its crudeness. Although *tamas* functions in its negative mode in most people, it becomes fragrant when melted by the fire of wisdom. In the case of the illumined personality of Christ, myrrh represents the unceasing flow of Divine Love and profound mental peace.

When a person lives a life of perpetual service to humanity, and thus learns to give all that he has for the welfare of humanity, he becomes a recipient of the unceasing inflow of Divine Grace and receives the infinite treasure of the Kingdom of Heaven. By the joyous momentum of renunciation, he attains Self-realization.

King Herod represents the impure ego, which is frightened to lose its power at the emergence of Divine Aspiration—Jesus Christ. It tries its utmost to destroy such aspiration by destroying the newborn babies, because it is afraid to lose its attachments to possessions, relationships with others, and worldly values. However, spiritual aspiration cannot be destroyed; it outgrows the time of Herod and his tyranny.

The three Sages do not return to Herod. The course of Nature, which was beholden to the king, now detaches itself from him and offers its gifts to Jesus. In other words, there is a transformation of energy. Impure ego is gradually deprived of Nature's gifts, and spiritual aspiration becomes the focus of one's life—the movement towards God.

The Genealogy of Christ

In the prelude to the Holy Gospel of Jesus Christ according to St. Matthew, Christ is said to be "the son of David, the son of Abraham." Then following in the genealogy is an enumeration of all the generations from Abraham to David and from David to Joseph, the father of Christ.

It is noteworthy that this portion of the New Testament refers to Christ as the son of David and Abraham, not the son of Adam. The "son of Adam" would imply an ordinary human being, one who has not undergone the necessary spiritual transformation to commune with God or establish a relationship with the Divinity. Abraham is a transformed son of Adam, a transformed human being. His personality illustrates the spiritual potentiality in man. An ordinary person is naturally related to Adam— the limited spirit struggling through the maze of desires. But an illumined personality establishes his relationship to God, the Divine Self. Since the Kingdom of Heaven is within every human being, such a relationship with God is possible for all through Enlightenment.

In Abraham, spiritual glory is more subjective, more mental and abstract; but in David, spiritual glory embraces the objective world as well. David symbolizes not only a process of inner transformation, but also an outer expression in the form of his royal elegance. Abraham and David, therefore, serve as two symbolic milestones on the way to the development of Jesus the Christ.

Christ symbolizes the blossoming of the Spirit in its most perfect manifestation. Within Him

dwell the potentiality and the introspection of Abraham, as well as the creative expression and splendor of David. Since these two factors are well integrated within his personality, Christ transcends them both.

The Virgin Mary and Joseph

Joseph is symbolic of the individual soul that has attained simplicity and purity. Prior to purification, the struggling souls of the world are wedded to a mind that is filled with worldly impressions. Therefore, their progeny take the form of worldly values—desires, cravings, attachments that never yield the ultimate joy and fulfillment.

However, Joseph was wedded to Mary, who symbolizes the higher, intuitive mind. The virginity of Mary is symbolic of her intrinsic purity. While for the worldly mind there are many realities to which it must be wedded, for the intuitive mind there is only one Reality. The intuitive mind does not perceive duality or differences in the homogeneous existence of the Absolute. It is the perception of duality that taints the spirit of man.

The individual soul, in its journey of evolution, comes in conjunction with the intuitive mind. Thus, spiritual aspiration is born. All worldly values are born through the ego and the lower mind; but in the birth of spiritual aspiration, the ego is gradually transcended.

Initially, Joseph was ashamed to reveal that Mary was with child. But when the Angel (Divine insight) informed him of the implications of Mary's conception, he was overjoyed. Such is the manner in which the ego of man comes to joyfully recognize a spiritual unfolding that must transcend and efface it—the mystical process of the birth of Christ, His growth, and final attainment.

The Meaning of Isaiah's Prophecy

Prophecies are symbolic of the Divine possibilities in human consciousness. These prophecies are not fulfilled as a historical development, but in the form of spiritual revelation and Divine realization within an aspirant. From this point of view, the Divine Birth in man has been prophesized in all religions of the world. But this birth necessitates the recovery of the pure state of the mind and the transcending of egoistic values. The Divine Birth is the revelation of what already exists as the Reality. Such revelation brings about a spiritual transformation in one's own consciousness and invokes a series of mystical developments in order to lead the soul from the realms of limitations and relativity to the realm of eternity and transcendence.

Isaiah implied that the Virgin Mind, intuition, would be revealed in the process of spiritual transformation. Such a Mind would commune with the Supreme Divinity. This intuitive state follows the manifestation of God in the consciousness of man in the form of spiritual aspiration. The Divine Son is called Immanuel (God is with us), because He points to the transcendent glory of the Self. Spiritual aspiration is in itself a glimpse of the essential Divinity within everyone; and the blossoming of such an aspiration implies a complete realization of the Divinity. Thus, the Divine Son leads one to the Heavenly Father—aspiration leads one to Liberation.

It is interesting to note that the Christian concept of the Trinity (Father, Son and Holy Ghost) is similar to the Vedantic concept of *Brahman* as Existence (*Sat*), Consciousness (*Chit*) and Bliss (*Ananda*). The Father possesses absolute power; He is the Supreme Existence behind all names and forms. The Son is the Embodiment of Absolute Consciousness or Knowledge, Who manifests to promote Enlightenment. The Holy Spirit is the Embodiment of Love, and therefore is characterized by limitless Bliss. In both Christian and Vedic mysticism, these Three are not separate, but united. It is the One expressing in Three.

The Way to Christ-Consciousness

With the understanding of the mystical symbolism implied in Christ's birth, an aspirant should not look forward in the distant future for Saviors to come, but he should create the circumstances of the Divine Birth within himself. When spiritual aspiration is born through purity of nature and integration of personality, the infinite beauty that is hidden within one's soul will gradually bloom within one's heart. The story of Christ will unfold within oneself. It will lead to the crucifixion, wherein the ego is transcended and reason is transformed into intuition. The movement towards the Kingdom of Heaven, the realization of the Cosmic Self, is the message of Christ's birth. And it is through prayer, meditation, and selfless activities that one worships Christ, invokes him within one's own being, and finally takes up the Cross to transcend the ego and enter into the Kingdom of Heaven, realizing one's union with the Supreme Self.

This is the way to Christ Consciousness, which is the same as Krishna Consciousness, Rama Consciousness, Cosmic Consciousness, and the *Nirvana* of the Buddha. It is the glorious goal of human existence.

The Crucifixion

Through His crucifixion, Lord Jesus teaches us about transformation in human personality. As we have seen, the Cross symbolizes the blending of two values—one human, dictated by ego, and the other Cosmic, based upon the vision that all is One.

The vision of unity towers over everything else and penetrates your very bones. You cannot be a separate individual even for a single moment. However, the problem with human existence is that it is defined by illusions; you constantly confine yourself to certain mental concepts. An individual soul in the state of ignorance resembles a frog that has hopped into a dark well and can't get out.

However, the pressure of the spirit within you propels you to break through the veils of illusion to emerge from the dark well of ignorance. In other words, in your everyday life you allow that Cosmic vision to pierce the crust of your egoistic vision. Symbolically speaking, egoistic vision is "crucified" by the Cosmic vision. If you understand this crucifixion, the world becomes a festivity.

When you begin to perceive the higher spiritual realms through spiritual practices, you begin to transcend the horizontal aspect of the Cross: being dependent on objects, people and circumstances within the world to fulfill your pursuit of happiness. Even when many or all of your dreams are fulfilled here on earth, eventually you are again left with the question: Where is the ultimate state of joy?

At that point, there is nowhere else to go. You have to follow the vertical direction of the Cross. Seeing the limitations woven within the objects and circumstances of time and space, you begin to pursue

oneness with God and unity with all life. With great patience, you move vertically by remembering who you really are—Divinity.

Some simple pictorial imagery may help you to better understand this idea. Consider, for example, you are a person who has wandered away from familiar surroundings and has gotten lost in a dense forest on a dark moonless night. Everywhere you turn you see ghosts and goblins. The very breeze that blows through the trees seems to sigh with grief. Somehow you must cope with the darkness until it passes. Only then will you be able to find your way home. But stumbling about in the darkness, trembling at an owl's staccato hoots, you consider this impossible and almost reconcile yourself to failure.

But then you wait and watch. The sun begins to rise and light streams through the dark clouds. The moment the first rays of light appear, the scene changes. Shadows that you thought were ghosts and goblins turn out to be lush trees decked with flowers. The giants that you beheld in the overpowering darkness were really mountain summits covered with silvery snow. The whole scene is transformed into a picturesque and inspiring setting.

Much in the same way, the gloom of ignorance can give way to the radiance of Liberation. Confined to your ego, you are bewildered as you stagger in the darkness of life's difficult situations. But once you transcend your ego through prayer and allow your spirit to discover just a single ray of the transcendental light of God, you find that the world is not as strange, terrible, or sorrowful as you had imagined. Rather every moment that you live, you feel sustained by Divine glory and surrounded by Divine majesty. The message of Christ's life is that you must discover that glory and majesty yourself. This is the implication of the teaching, *"Take up the Cross and follow me"* (KJV Mark 10:21):

> **If any man will come after Me, let him deny himself, and take up his Cross, and follow Me. For whosoever will save his life shall lose it: and whosoever will lose his life for My sake shall find it.**
> (KJV Matthew 16: 24-25)

Taking up the Cross is a constant effort to let go of the illusions that one's ego has created. You are not here on this earth to live for your ego. You are living to see that your ego dissolves.

Through His crucifixion, Christ symbolizes the effacement of ego and presents that attainment as a great challenge to all spiritual aspirants. As you purify your reason and learn to introspect deeply, you begin to see how many egoistic illusions and irrational thoughts abide within the mind. Due to the pressure of ego and an erroneous sense of individuality, so many negative impediments develop in life. Hatred, greed and selfishness torture human relationships and cause chaos within the world.

As you go on sacrificing your egoistic attitudes with vigilance and valor, you constantly affirm the Cross. If you only pursue the individualized, physical life of your personality, you gain nothing. But if you stop clinging to individuality—a development that is possible in the state of Enlightenment, you gain eternal life. This is what Jesus implied when he spoke to his disciples about taking up the Cross.

According to Raja Yoga, there are five *kleshas*, or afflictions of the unconscious: *avidya, asmita, raga, dwesha,* and *abhinivesha. Avidya* is ignorance. Out of ignorance arises *asmita*, or egoism. Egoism sets up two currents: *raga* and *dwesha*, or attachment and hatred. These create karmic entanglements causing one to become attached to one's physical life. This attachment or "clinging" to physical life is called *abhinivesha*. These kleshas are eradicated when one takes up the Cross.

The vertical movement of transcending ego negates the horizontal movement of a life steeped in ignorance. This uplifting movement is the secret of bearing the Cross in your everyday life. Instead of perpetuating the same egoistic vision of life, caught in the repetitive boredom of sensual enjoyments, include the vertical, transcendental movement wherein you learn to love God by serving Him in humanity. Meditate on His Divine Nature. Realize, "I am He." Thus, enter into the everlasting festivity of the Kingdom of Heaven—the blissful realm of *Nirvana*.

The Resurrection of Lord Jesus

Man's triumph over death, though presented in various ways, is the most important theme of all the world's religions. The resurrection of Christ celebrated on Easter Sunday is the commemoration of Christ's triumph over death and is, therefore, an event of supreme importance for all mankind.

In the light of Vedanta philosophy, the resurrection of Christ is symbolic of the attainment of Liberation. As an aspirant progresses on the spiritual path, an inner transformation occurs, described symbolically in the Gospel of St. Matthew:

And, behold, there was a great earthquake: for the angel of the Lord descended from heaven, and came and rolled back the stone from the door, and sat upon it. His countenance was like lightning, and his raiment white as snow.

(KJV Matthew 28: 2-3)

The earthquake symbolizes the upheaval of the unconscious as impure impressions are propelled to the surface and replaced by pure impressions. The Angel of the Lord is symbolic of intuitive vision. Rolling back the stone refers to the removal of bondage (in the form of ignorance), while the snow and lightning suggest purity and revelation.

The very being of Lord Jesus passes through the process of crucifixion so that He might be resurrected as the Spiritual Being that blends with the Heavenly Father. Spiritual aspiration grows into the state of intuitional vision, which crucifies ego-consciousness and sentimental attachments to the world and resurrects the soul from the world of death and mortality. Thus resurrected, the soul realizes its essential identity with the Divine Self and attains the Kingdom of Heaven.

Thus, in Vedanta, the resurrection is symbolic of the attainment of *Jivan Mukti* or Liberation in life. In Christian terms, Lord Jesus ascended to the Kingdom of Heaven to be united with the resurrected body. Vedantically speaking, He realized His identity with the Absolute Self and became free of the cycles of birth and death.

The Imperishability of the Human Spirit

The resurrection of Christ shows that He is incorruptible: He does not perish. He was tortured and crucified and His body was secured behind a rock—and yet He rose again. Whether or not one believes that Christ literally rose from the dead does not matter. One can still be thrilled by that miracle as a testimony to the taintlessness and the incorruptibility of the Spirit within us all.

Lord Jesus was established in the awareness that He was not the body, but Spirit. The same is true of Kabira, a 15th century Saint of India. He had two types of followers, Hindu and Mohammedan. When he died, both claimed his body. The Mohammedans wanted to bury his body, considering him to be their Guru, and the Hindus wanted to cremate him, considering him to be their Guru. A great quarrel ensued. After a while, one of them lifted the shroud covering the dead body and found that it was gone; what remained were only flowers. So it was easy to reconcile the argument—half the flowers went to the Hindus for cremation and half went to the Mohammedans for burial.

Aspirants become firmly rooted in this understanding when they realize that they have two types of birth. One is the normal birth, which terminates in death. The other is the spiritual birth, which commences when you enter the spiritual path. Being born spiritually, you conquer death, because you are no longer the body. That is the message of the resurrection. The potential to resurrect dwells within every human being, and every Sage reminds you of that potential. Deep within lies the incorruptible Self, the taintless Spirit, the pure *Atman*, and you can realize that *Atman* even within this lifetime.

The Judgment Day—The Second Coming of Christ

Christianity describes the Judgment Day as the time when virtuous souls enter the Kingdom of Heaven and enjoy everlasting Bliss, while vicious souls are thrown into the eternal fires of hell. Lord Jesus relates in St. Matthew (12:36), *"But I say unto you, that every idle word that men shall speak, they shall give account thereof in the day of judgment."* This statement indicates that every karma (action performed by thought, word or deed) is judged by a Divine Law. Virtue brings its reward through happiness and prosperity, and vice bears its fruit through pain and misery.

The highest judgment, however, is the attainment of that state wherein every soul is eternally free of the relativity of virtue and vice. Therefore, the Judgment Day implies the attainment of Liberation, characterized by the ultimate victory of the forces of light and the annihilation of the forces of darkness.

From an esoteric point of view, the Judgment Day does not take place during a specific point in time, but can occur for an individual at any time.

According to Vedanta, this occurs in the state of *Jivan Mukti* or Liberation in life. It is the state of Enlightenment. The true spirit of religion is not waiting for the second coming of Christ at some future date, but accepting that manifestation within one's own heart even within one's lifetime.

Chapter Twenty

Christ Consciousness Healing the World

Today, in spite of the brilliant discoveries made by science and unimaginable technological advancements, there is a continuing tendency towards violence, stress and insecurity everywhere in the world. On one side, man has proven his unimaginable brilliance through scientific explorations into the mysteries of matter, while on the other side, his unconscious mind and his heart continue to be as uncultured as they were during the dark ages of the past.

This being the case, human progress can be compared to what happens when a galloping horse speeds towards the west, while his ignorant rider is all the while seated towards the east! Due to his ignorance, the rider is so excited with the speed of the horse and the power behind its gallops that he is unaware of his miserable predicament; while the rider thinks that he is riding faster and faster towards

his destination, he is actually moving further and further away from it!

While human beings are awed by the extremely powerful weapons that they have developed to express their anger and hatred, they have very little insight into what direction this is taking them. They do not understand how to sublimate negative sentiments and how to experience inner love and tranquility, thus uniting themselves with all humanity and all creation. People are dazzled by the amazing power of the nuclear bomb, but they are unaware of a far greater power that lies within their own reach—the power of the Spirit that can be awakened and unfolded in the stillness of their own heart. This is illustrated by the inspirational candle of Christ still burning today. Centuries have rolled by, and yet the power within the heart of Lord Jesus represented by His tender hands folded in prayer and devotion continues to work wonders. The dynamic forces of Divine Love emanating from His Being continue to inspire faith, courage and undaunted heroism in all those who have spiritual sensitivity.

Cleansing the Temple of the Human Heart

Not long before the festival of Passover, Jesus went to Jerusalem. There He found people selling cattle, sheep, and doves in the temple. He also saw moneychangers sitting at their tables. So He took some rope and made a whip. Then He chased everyone out of the temple, together with their sheep and cattle. He turned over the tables of the moneychangers and scattered their coins. (CEV John 2:13—16)

The root-cause of all the disharmony and restlessness of today is the fact that the temple of the human heart has become an abode of "money-changers." It has been defiled by the impressions generated on the basis of egoism, attachment, hatred, and infatuation. The human heart, which ought to be a seat of Divine impressions, has become a seat of the satanic qualities of pride, cruelty, hypocrisy, falsehood and greed. The doves of higher values are sold for petty material gains. Spiritual grace is sold for perishable rewards on the earth. Prayer is conditioned by egoistic demands. Surrender to God is replaced by hypocritical humility.

This state of affairs must change. For this temple of the heart to be restored to its original sanity, *chitta shuddhi* (purity of the heart) must be promoted. Lord Jesus—the Divine Aspiration in man—must gather the small cords of mental thought-waves and convert them into the whip of *viveka* (discriminative reason). With this whip of *viveka*, an aspirant can dispel the impurities that defile the Divine Temple. Without *chitta shuddhi*, it is not possible to enjoy real peace and harmony within oneself or in the world outside.

Chapter Twenty-One
Lord Jesus
The Embodiment of
Spiritual Majesty

Lord Jesus is the perfect mirror reflecting the boundless glory of the Absolute, the embodiment of the spiritual ideal of perfection that should be attained by every individual. To live a life of spiritual majesty and reveal to people what can be accomplished through human embodiment has always been the project of Saints, Sages, or Divine Incarnations. Jesus lived that life of inner majesty, and in so doing, directed our vision to the goal of life: attainment of the Kingdom of Heaven, *Nirvana*, *Moksha*, Liberation or God-realization. Although these are known by different names to different people, this glorious attainment is exactly the same.

Due to the misunderstanding of religion and spirituality, however, people are not fascinated by the goal of attaining the Kingdom of Heaven. Therefore, the task before every spiritual teacher is to reveal that Liberation is not something external to one's life, but rather, internal. It is the path to Liberation that begins to make life truly meaningful; and it is the attainment of Liberation that culminates in absolute and sublime joy.

As an illustration, imagine that you live in a house on a wonderful scenic hill. However, for years you have kept your windows permanently boarded up. If you were to remove the boards and open the windows, you would be able to enjoy the forest blazing with wonderful colors and the vast expansion of nature in all directions. The delightful fragrances would enter your home. But not realizing this, you hold onto your resolve out of fear and keep the windows closed.

Now suppose someone who observed the beautiful forests and magnificent flowers surrounding your home were to knock at your door and say, "Come out! At least open a window and see the wondrous beauty you have right outside!" But you are so involved with painting what you imagine to be scenes of nature in the comfort of your air-conditioned home that you reply, "Why should I open the windows and doors? How could anything be better than what I have here? It would only expose me to drafts and the cold bleak atmosphere. So why should I?"

However, a day does arrive when you become convinced that there must be something more, something better. So you decide to open a window, but just a small one, and just slightly. Lo and behold! The sight is so amazing it awes your mind. That vision now begins to inspire you to open more windows and to finally remove the boards so that you are able to view nature from every direction inside your home.

A fairytale transformation has taken place. No longer are you confined to the imaginary visions of nature. You have actually experienced it—the grandeur of the forest and flowers, the exhilarating, crisp, fresh air and the vast sky. You even take walks in the forest among the majestic trees enjoying the beautiful woodland creatures. You are now inspired to share your joy with others who remain locked up in their little prisons as you once were.

This figurative description applies to the life of Lord Jesus. He experienced the beauty of universality and eternity. He experienced the Kingdom of Heaven, unity with the Father, Oneness with God. Lord Jesus gave His Divine teachings so that everyone who listened might also open a window to eternity and experience the Kingdom of Heaven; and the same has been done by all Sages and Saints in all religions and on all spiritual paths of the world.

Following is a humorous parable to help you understand the dilemma in life that distracts many from the spiritual path: Once a group of thieves snuck into a dilapidated temple because they had been informed that hidden somewhere within this temple were treasures. Seeing a small hole as they entered, the leader placed his hand inside to see if there were any valuables. Instead of discovering a treasure, he was stung by a scorpion. However, being the leader and not wanting to lose face before the others, he shook his hand, and as he moved on, said, "What a wonderful experience!" One by one his followers all did the very same thing: reached inside the hole, received a painful sting, shook their hand, and said, "What a wonderful experience!"

Similarly, a person who has become very wealthy may create the impression before others that he is enjoying life abundantly; but actually, this is not so. Dissatisfied with the emptiness of wealth, a rich person may then decide he would be happy if he had power. So using his money he tries to enter into politics to acquire power and recognition. When at last the desired power is attained, he eventually realizes that it did not bring him the happiness he expected. Nevertheless, because of all the money and effort it took for him to attain that power, and also to keep up appearances, his pride spurs him on to continue bragging and advising others on how to attain success in life.

The implication here is that you may acquire wealth, power, relationships, etc., but these worldly attainments will never genuinely provide the ultimate fulfillment of joy you are searching for. Therefore, the Kingdom of Heaven should be your primary focus. For if you have Liberation as your goal, everything in your life will have value and significance. If Liberation is not your goal, then none of these attainments, after a time, will have any lasting meaning. You will eventually have the experience of emptiness. You will be like those hypocritical thieves, shaking their hands after being stung by the illusions of life, yet asserting, "What a wonderful experience!"

A mathematical illustration given by a teacher in India may help you understand this point from a different perspective: If you have worldly attainments without the aspiration for God-realization, then all you have are zeros. In mathematics, whether you have one zero or a thousand zeros, it still amounts to zero—nothing. But, if you place just a single "1" in front of the zeros, you give value to whatever zeros you have. One zero becomes 10, two zeros become 100, three zeros become 1,000, etc. Every zero has meaning and significance. Similarly, if you do not have the Kingdom of Heaven, God, before the "zeros" in your life, all your attainments are in vain. Aspire for the Kingdom of Heaven, and every attainment, every little accomplishment in your life will have a meaning and a purpose.

About the Author,
Swami Jyotirmayananda

S wami Jyotirmayananda was born on February 3, 1931, in Bihar, India, a northern province sanctified by the great Lord Buddha. In 1953, Swamiji embraced the ancient order of *sanyasa* as a disciple of Sri Swami Sivananda, the founder of the Divine Life Society, Rishikesh, India.

In tireless service to his Guru, Swamiji taught at the Yoga Vedanta Forest Academy, giving lectures on the Upanishads, Raja Yoga, Yoga Vasistha and other scriptures of India. Swamiji also handled all of Swami Sivananda's correspondence, translated many of his books into Hindi and served as the editor of the *Yoga Vedanta Journal*.

After many requests, Swami Jyotirmayananda came to the West in 1962 to spread the knowledge of Yoga and Vedanta philosophy. In 1969 he established the Ashram in Miami, Florida, which has become the center for the international activities of the Yoga Research Foundation.

In 1985, Swamiji established the International Yoga Society and the Divya Jyoti School for children in Loni near New Delhi, India. In 2000, the Jyotirmayananda Ashram and Vocational Training Center for abused and neglected women was established in Bihar, India. In 2006 the Lalita-Jyoti Anaathaalaya, an orphanage and school, opened its doors to 80 girls in Sonipat. These institutions in India are serving the community by offering regular *satsang*, Yoga classes, and periodic Yoga camps, as well as by translating Swamiji's writings to be published in Hindi and operating free medical clinics.

Today, Swami Jyotirmayananda occupies a place of the highest order among international men of wisdom. He is recognized as one of the foremost proponents of Integral Yoga, a way of life and thought that synthesizes the various aspects of the ancient Yoga tradition into a comprehensive plan of personality integration.

Through regular lectures and retreats in the Ashram, his books on all aspects of Yoga and Vedanta, and the monthly *International Yoga Guide* magazine, Swamiji continues to share the richness of his vast knowledge of the great scriptures of India and the world—tirelessly inspiring spiritual seekers everywhere to attain the true goal of life—Enlightenment.

BOOKS BY SWAMI JYOTIRMAYANANDA

Vedic Prayers and Mantras

Mantra Shiromani—Crest-Jewels of Mantra

Integral Yoga—The Secret to Enlightenment

The Art of Positive Thinking

The Art of Positive Feeling

Advice to Householders

Advice to Students

The Glory of Lord Krishna—Mysticism of Srimad Bhagavatam

Mysticism of the Mahabharata

The Way to Liberation (Mahabharata), 2 Vols.

Mysticism of the Ramayana

Worship of God as Mother—Mysticism of Devi Mahatmya

Concentration and Meditation

Applied Yoga

Death and Reincarnation

Raja Yoga — Study of Mind

Yoga Exercises for Health and Happiness

Beauty and Health through Yoga Relaxation

Yoga Can Change Your Life

Yoga Vasistha, 6 Vols.

The Mystery of the Soul—(Katha Upanishad)

Yoga Wisdom of the Upanishads

Raja Yoga Sutras

Yoga Secrets of Psychic Powers

Sex-Sublimation, Truth and Non-Violence

Yoga of Perfection (Srimad Bhagavad Gita)

Yoga of Enlightenment (Srimad Bhagavad Gita—Chapter 18)

Srimad Bhagavad Gita (pocket edition)

Vedanta in Brief

The Yoga of Divine Love (Narada Bhakti Sutras)

Jnana Yoga (Yoga Secrets of Wisdom)

Mantra, Kirtana, Yantra, and Tantra

Hindu Gods and Goddesses

Yoga Guide

Yoga Quotations

Yoga Mystic Poems

Yoga Mystic Stories

Yoga Stories and Parables

Waking, Dream and Deep Sleep

Yoga Essays for Self-Improvement

Integral Yoga Today

For a comprehensive list of books and digital media offered by the Yoga Research Foundation, please visit the online store at www.shop.yrf.org.

CPSIA information can be obtained
at www.ICGtesting.com
Printed in the USA
FSOW01n1719160218
44416FS